Contents

PHOTO CREDITS

The photographs of Traute Ishida's rugs were taken by her husband, the photographs of rugs by Marla Mallett, Bruce Duderstadt, Gloria Crouse, and Sarah Harkness and the rugs in the "Grown in Idaho" series by Michel Little were taken by the craftsmen themselves. The rugs by Hildegarde Klene were photographed by José Bermudez, those of John Adolph were photographed by Jules Kliot, proprietor of Some Place, a store in Berkeley, California. The photographs of the Mills-Mosseller rugs were taken by T. Mosseller. The rug patterns are courtesy of Heirloom Rugs and Wilson Brothers. The photographs of the rag tapestries, "The Beginning of the Beginning" and "New York," were photographed by Katrina Thomas. The details were also photographed by Ms. Thomas, except for one photographed by Charles Fish. "Tamarac Tiger" was photographed by John Gaylord, and "Leopard Family" was photographed by Margaret Norton.

The photographs of the latch hooked rugs designed by artists for Rufus and Leslie Stillman were photographed by John T. Hill and John A. Ferrari and are courtesy of the Stephen Radich Gallery, New York.

The photograph of the latch hooked Calder rug in the Stillman's bedroom was taken by Joe Ribar. All equipment and "how-to" photographs were taken by Naomi Bushman.

My appreciation is extended to all the photographers represented in this book.

FIRST EDITION

Designed by Lydia Link

Library of Congress Cataloging in Publication Data
Cuyler, Susanna.
  The high-pile rug book.
  Bibliography: p.
  1. Hooking, 2. Rugs, Hooked. 3. Rya rugs.
I. Title.
TT850.C88 1974   746.7′4   73–4074
ISBN 0–06–010936–X

RUG BOOK

Susanna Cuyler

HARPER & ROW, PUBLISHERS
New York, Evanston, San Francisco, London

THE HIGH-PILE

THE HIGH-PILE RUG BOOK

Acknowledgments

This book owes its existence to the contributions of many rugmakers. I wish to express gratitude to my aunt, Leslie Stillman, whose latch hooked rugs first interested me in rugs; to George Wells, who knows more about rug hooking techniques than anyone, and who introduced me to work of Gloria F. Ross, Hildegarde Klene, and Gloria Finn; to Jules Kliot for his information on rugmaking in California; and to Ann Wiseman, whose rag tapestries have contributed to the interest in rugs today.

I wish to thank those who freely and willingly gave me their professional advice: George Wells, Leslie Stillman, Stephen Radich, and Ann Wiseman.

I am deeply grateful to the craftsmen represented in the Research and Education Department's files at the American Craftsmen's Council for their contribution of photographs and information about their work. In particular, my correspondence with Evelyn Anselevicius, Traute Ishida, and Lillian Mills-Mosseller has been rewarding.

To the American Crafts Council, 44 West 53rd Street, New York City, I owe a great debt. Their library files have been invaluable in the preparation of this book.

And to Joe Ribar, who is responsible for my living in Claverack, New York, where it was possible for me to write this book.

Fig. 1 Hooked textures by George Wells.

Introduction

Crafts are skills that when successfully applied produce objects that are both beautiful and functional. Rugmaking is one such craft. The best incentive for making your own rug is to shop for one in a good store. You will see that mass-produced rugs are simplistic in design, have limited colors, and are usually outrageously expensive. A handmade rug, however, costs less and has a custom-tailored design and color scheme.

In primitive societies crafts are the result of necessity. Necessity leads to inventiveness and subsequently to artistic excellence. In Africa, for instance, artistic excellence is maintained because of a tradition of handing down the best examples of craftsmanship for younger craftsmen to equal or surpass.

In semi-industrialized countries, such as Mexico and India, crafts contribute to both the national culture and economy. In both of these countries the balance of industrialization and the production of handicrafts was conscientiously achieved. Traditional methods and designs had to be reinforced to enable Indian and rural Mexican communities to survive financially, maintain their cultural heritage, and attract due interest from tourists.

In nations where crafts and craft-makers are allowed to retain their cultural importance, they add immeasurably to the country's well-being. A case could be made that a nation's morale and its countrymen's mental health can be ascribed to the government's success in balancing arts and crafts with its mass-produced items.

Sweden has actively promoted crafts both as a source of revenue and as a means of national expression. The government of the United States never fully supported crafts. This was partly due to our emergence as a nation during the industrial revolution. But when a government does not encourage its national crafts, at least it should not forget them. If a government neglects crafts while supporting industry, crafts become lost. With only a slight degree of federal support, American crafts can grow into an important national cultural expression, a source of revenue, and an attraction to the peoples of other countries.

A particular craft that has been excluded from federal concern and suppressed by industry is rug tufting. Rug tufting is a term applied to pile rugs with a cut-even surface. A Georgia farm girl, Catherine Evans, invented tufting while sewing a "tuft" on a bedspread in 1895. During the next ten years, she tufted and sold bedspreads to friends and to stores. When she had too many orders, she traveled in her buggy and taught neighbors to tuft, bringing them the materials and returning to pick up the finished bedspreads, bathrobes, and rugs. Twenty-five years later sewing machines capable of tufting were introduced but, in 1930, there were still 10,000 hand tufters.

After World War II, high-speed tufting machines were developed and introduced to corporate manufacturers. Wool replaced cotton yarn, and subsequently synthetic yarns replaced wool. Synthetics were necessary to withstand the extreme pressure of the tufting machines. Industrialization became so extensive that, in 1969, 564 million square yards of tufted carpeting was produced, exceeding the output of the stable woven-carpet industry.

The American public has now recognized the imbalance between industry and crafts, the rape of crafts by industry. The result has been a revived interest in crafts. During the last decade, an increasing number of people have bought handicrafts, made things themselves, or read about a variety of crafts. Excluding the personal satisfaction involved, the resurgence of crafts is attributable to the better quality and lower price when compared with their mass-produced counterparts. The primary reason for mass production—quality at an inexpensive price—has, in many areas, become self-defeating.

New economic and cultural advantages from crafts have begun to be realized. A great effort in Appalachia, similar to the one in Mexico, rejuvenated traditional crafts and introduced new ones. With government subsidies, Appalachian craft workshops and cooperatives were organized and are now virtually self-sustaining. The economic advantage of crafts in impoverished communities has been tested and proven effective. Besides supplying the existing handicraft market, the production of handicrafts is adjustable to the talents and time of the various participants. In craft cooperatives craftsmen can learn, acquire materials at discount prices, work with other craftsmen, have a source of income from workshop contracts, and use the place as an outlet for their own projects. Craftsmen have never enjoyed the benefits of most workers, such as organized marketing procedures, stabilized incomes, and group insurance. But through cooperatives, craftsmen can at least have more leverage in production and marketing.

Craft fairs, exhibitions, and stores provide selling outlets for the majority of craftsmen. At a craft fair a craftsman, while becoming better acquainted with the competition, more than likely is able to sell his work and take orders for future projects. Presently, the main craft fairs are the League of New Hampshire Arts and Crafts Fair, held in August; the Mountain State Art and Craft Fair, held near Ripley, West Virginia, during the Fourth of July week; the American Folklife Festival in Washington, D.C., also held during the Fourth of July week; the Northeast Fair sponsored by the American Crafts Council; and the Craftsmen Fair of the Southern Highlands, held in July in Asheville, North Carolina, and in October in Gatlinburg, Tennessee.

The arts councils of California, Missouri, Georgia, Illinois, Washington, Oregon, and Tennessee offer assistance with craft exhibitions and information on additional events throughout the state. The Farmers' Cooperative Service and the Farmers' Home Administration Extension Service, connected with the Department of Agriculture, offer assistance for the rural craftsman wishing to supplement his income. The Economic Development Administration of the Department of Commerce has been very successful with the cooperative projects in West Virginia. The Smithsonian Institution and other museums have had exhibits and maintain craft shops. The American Crafts Council in New York City has been invaluable in promoting crafts through the magazine *Craft Horizons,* the Museum of Contemporary Crafts, and its library where craftsmen keep files of their work.

There are three different kinds of craftsmen: traditional craftsmen who make objects from handed-down designs, artist-craftsmen who make one-of-a-kind objects, and designer-craftsmen who design an object for other craftsmen to make.

Most of the craftsmen represented in this book are artist-craftsmen. Several designer-craftsmen have found a very workable arrangement in rugmaking. The working conditions are adjustable and it is financially feasible to pay other craftsmen. A rug can also be made by a group. A number of people can work together without the finished product looking as though many fingers had gone into the pie.

The artistic and technical possibilities of the rug medium are encouraged by new equipment and techniques that help craftsmen work quickly and achieve new effects. Recently there have been several art gallery shows of rugs designed by artists, sculptors, and architects; "paintings in wool" exhibited with the original oil paintings; tapestry translations of modern painters' work; and mural-like tapestries made by children and hung in museums and schools.

The artistic and technical advice given in this book is intended to make rugmaking a realizable craft for the reader.

Misconceptions about the time, cost, and work involved in rugmaking have arisen from the assumption that projects as large as rugs must require a lot of time, equipment, work, and materials. But this is not true. It is the purpose of this book to dispel these misconceptions. The techniques described make rugmaking both enjoyable and profitable, and can serve to elevate the ancient craft to a new level.

Susanna Cuyler

Fig. 2 Punch needle wall hanging by Silvia Heyden.

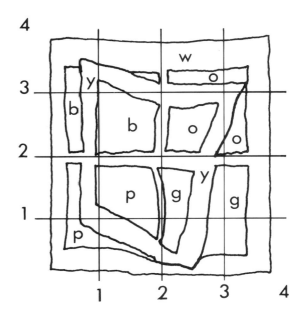

There are two principles that apply to the forms of rugmaking described in this book. The first is that clarity of line and color differentiation are determined by the height of the pile. A short zigzag line is sharply defined in a 1/4-inch pile but is lost in a pile higher than an inch. The shorter the pile, the denser it must be so that the backing does not show through. Oriental carpets are constructed with a knotted pile that is approximately 1/8 inch high, with several hundred knots per square inch to clarify the complicated design. These carpets are very beautiful, but to make one of them is a massive project. Only rugmakers working in groups, for thousands of hours, are able to make them by hand.

The techniques described in this book can produce details that are distinguishable when viewed from the distances at which rugs and wall hangings are usually viewed. But they can never have the complexity of detail found in a woven Oriental carpet. There are as few as three knots to a square inch in a rya; a line is produced that is equivalent to a thick chalk line. Extremely fine color gradations are possible, however, because the pile is comprised of very thin strands of yarn.

A latch hooked rug has a maximum of sixteen knots per square inch and a pile that is always higher than 3/4 inch. The clarity of design is equivalent to that of lines drawn with a crayon or a watercolor brush. A hooked rug has up to thirty loops per square inch, which permits the finest detail of all the techniques. A clear even line can be hooked that is equivalent to a line drawn with a felt-tip pen.

The higher the pile, the less definition of line. No detail is distinct in a thick shaggy pile rug because of the proportion of pattern line to the height and shagginess of the pile.

The second consideration for pile rugs is that of texture. A rug's surface is three dimensional. When the pile is uneven, the contrast of texture is more obvious. Looped pile makes the texture knobbly, and the higher the loops, the coarser the grain. However, the pile

Fig. 1-2 Line clarity is determined by the height of the pile. On the left is a sketch for a 6-inch-square face. On the right is the face hooked in a 1/2-inch pile. This face would be difficult to recognize in a 1-inch pile and would be the most distinct in a 1/4-inch pile.

can be cut so that the texture of the rug is unobtrusive. Cut pile with a density of twenty-five loops per square inch will look more uniform than the pile of a latch hooked rug which has a maximum density of sixteen knots per square inch.

There are both hooked and knotted rug techniques illustrated in this book. In a hooked rug the pile is pushed or pulled through a backing; in a knotted rug the yarn is knotted to the backing.

The pile is formed in rows of loops in a hooked rug. When a hand hook is used, the loops are pulled up individually through the weave of the cloth to any height the rugmaker desires. With a speed hook, the pile is pushed down through the backing and the height of the loops is adjustable to set heights from 1/4 inch to 1 1/2 inches. Speed hooking is the fastest method of rugmaking. There are three varieties of speed hooks: the punch needle, the shuttle hook, and the speed tufting tool. The last two are the fastest methods because they automatically space the loops.

There are two different types of knotted rugmaking techniques. The latch hook method uses cut yarn that is folded and knotted onto a stiff mesh backing that has a uniform number of mesh holes per square inch. The pile is cut and knotted, and can be of almost any height. In the rya, the pile is knotted in elongated loops that lie flat on the backing. This is the only technique in which the pile is long but lies flat. The rya yarn is especially thin and twisted so that the ends will not unravel when they are cut.

Despite the diversity of methods employed to make these rugs and the varying appearances when finished, the techniques are similar in the amount of yarn used, time involved, and total cost.

On the average, a half pound of wool yarn or material is used per square foot for either a knotted or hooked 1-inch pile rug.

Rugmaking equipment is inexpensive. The cost of rug yarn fluctuates. The average price is five dollars a pound, and a pound will cover two square feet. For hooked rugs, old clothes and blankets and other scraps that cost little or nothing can be used. This will diminish your expenses considerably.

Table 1
Comparative Rugmaking Techniques

Technique	Average hours per sq. ft.	Material used per sq. ft.	Extra equipment needed
Hooking			
hand hook	$4\frac{1}{2}$	$\frac{1}{2}$ lb.	—
punch hook	1	$\frac{1}{2}$ lb.	frame
shuttle hook	$\frac{3}{4}$	$\frac{1}{2}$ lb.	frame
tufting tool	$\frac{1}{2}$	$\frac{1}{2}$ lb.	frame
Knotting			
latch hook	$4\frac{1}{2}$	$\frac{1}{2}$ lb.	—
rya	3	$\frac{1}{2}$ lb.	—

Fig. 1-3 "Tamarac Tiger," shuttle hooked by Ann Wiseman.

Table 2
Amount of Wool Yarn Used for
Hooking Different Pile Heights

Pile	Per 6 sq. in.	Per sq. ft.	Sq. ft. per lb.
¼ in.	1 oz.	4 oz.	4
½ in.	1½ oz.	6 oz.	2½+
1 in.	1¾ oz.	7 oz.	2¼

Using 6-inch squares hooked at different heights with separate 4 oz. balls of wool yarn, I found the above computations to be true.

A speed hooked rug can be completed by an experienced rugmaker at the rate of one square foot per half hour. The time, however, depends on the amount of details, changes of color and height of pile, as well as the rugmaker's manual dexterity. A square foot can be latch hooked in four to five hours. With rya it takes approximately three hours, and with a hand hook a rugmaker may complete a square foot in four to five hours.

The principal difference between a rug that you make and one that you buy in a store is in the manner of production and the materials used. Commercially tufted and pile rugs are manufactured by machines that have several thousand needles attached to bars through which yarn is pumped. The backing of the rug is stretched flat under the fast-moving needles. This procedure requires very strong yarn, which means that synthetic fibers must be used. Although they are very strong, they lack the soft luxurious feel of good wool. The fastest commercial method of printing a pattern on a tufted or pile rug uses a rotating cylinder. The dyes are kept inside the drum and applied to the rug as the cylinder is rotated. Another method, less often used, is to print a design through a number of screens, one for each color. The screens are held on a rigid frame with a fine mesh. The parts of the screen where color is not to go through are coated. This method is called silk screening.

If the designs are not stamped on in some way, then the rug is dipped into an enormous dye bath after it is made, or the synthetic yarns are dyed in a solution before the tufting begins.

By making your own rugs you can use wool yarn or other soft materials that are not only durable and resilient but also soft to the touch. These rugs will last for generations and can be designed to suit yourself. Even a plain rug of one color is beautiful when it is handmade.

Rugs, wall hangings, pillows, clothes, and even slipcovers and sculptures can be made in any of the pile techniques. I simply use the word *rug* because it refers to the basic form from which the others arise.

I suggest that you first try a method that is best suited to your immediate requirements. Let the size of the project depend on the choice of design.

I am confident that rugmaking will give you many good times.

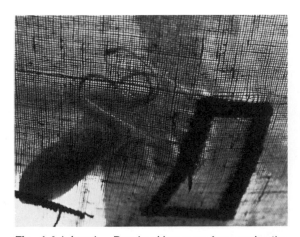

Fig. 1-4 (*above*)   Rug hooking seen from under the frame. The point of a speed hook is visible.

Fig. 1-5   The original design for a rug by Antonio Frasconi, printed on tissue paper.

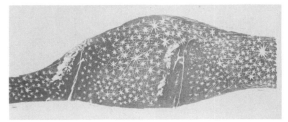

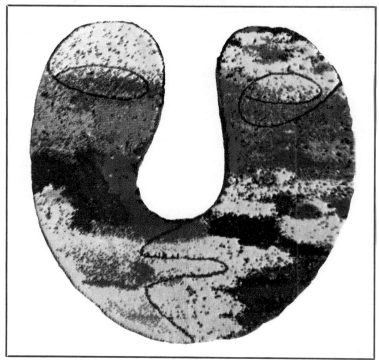

Plate 1 (*left*) Latch hooked rug by Traute Ishida.

Plate 2 Completed latch hooked rug (46″ × 48″), designed by Antonio Frasconi in 1966.

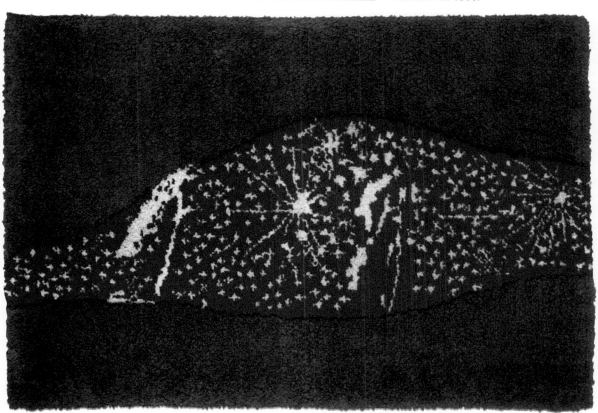

2

Rug Design and Color

Rug Design

Wall hangings can be compared to paintings and tapestries can be compared to murals, but a rug cannot really be compared to anything. A rug is seen from above. It is seen from various angles and at changing distances; therefore the figures or shapes on the side of the rug farthest away from you are foreshortened.

Furniture either surrounds a rug or is placed on it; dogs can obstruct the design when they lie on the rug, also people stand, walk, and sit on it. In the daylight the rug may look completely different from the way it looks at night when lights shine on it.

Because of these properties, the rug is an obvious place for color and design. The pliable surface is ideal for textural variations. The soft cushioning features of a rug make it unlike any other source of aesthetic or sensual pleasure.

If the beginner has difficulty in choosing a design, a possible approach is to divide the sketch into blocks. Each block can then be worked on until a design has been formed. In antiquity many homeowners did just this. They divided their floor space with crossing lines and filled the blocks in a logical sequence. There are many other ways of approaching rug design, but the fundamental concepts of consistency, balance, and simplicity should persist.

The simpler the design, the better it can be transferred to a rug. If a design is only interesting to look at from one angle, and the rug is to be looked at from several directions, the design will not be as effective.

The size of the design deserves careful consideration. If the design is cluttered with too many images, too many contrasts, and not enough balance between light and dark areas, it may not serve well as a rug design. But don't be afraid to explore any design. If a design is not suited to a rug, it could make a stunning wall hanging.

Any design can be converted into a rug or wall hanging, both technically and legally. Pictures can be exactly copied, or vaguely adapted, because the design will be reproduced in a different medium than that originally used by the artist. For example, if you copy a Picasso painting it is not literally a copy because the materials you use are yarn and not paints. It is only fair, however, to call the rug or wall hanging after the name of the copied painting, or in some way indicate the source of the adaptation. If an artist designs a rug, this design is the artist's and he can protect it with a copyright.

Certain effects peculiar to other mediums, such as shiny surfaces or highly reflective ones, cannot really be reproduced in a rug. It is possible, though, to reproduce general brush strokes, paint splatters, bright and subtle light sources, fine shading, and pointillism.

If possible, the size of the design should be

Fig. 2-1 Rya rug by Reba Maisel.

relative to the size of the room. A rug should be part of the decoration; its color scheme and subject matter must be in harmony with the rest of the room. Walking on a rug depicting a surrealistic landscape gives one a very different feeling from that of walking on a rug depicting a sensuous nude.

Sources of rug designs are unlimited. Fine examples are found in quilt patterns, crewel embroidery, tiles, aerial and scientific photographs, collages, line drawings, and especially paintings.

Choose a design because it is balanced and has interesting contrasts. Like a painting, a rug design is most effective if its parts relate well to one another. A light area looks lighter if there is a dark area surrounding it. A flyaway shape will become more anchored when it is enclosed in a border. A circle seems larger if there are dots near it in the composition. (The dots serve to create an optical illusion.) Direc-

Fig. 2-2 "The Punjab Tryst" (7' × 3'), hooked with a Susan Burr hook by Ann Wiseman. Commissioned by H. Fox, Princeton, N.J.

tional contrasts like stars and arrows are good elements to include in a rug design because they are recognizable from all sides of the rug. Other contrasts are long and short, wide and narrow, smooth and rough, soft and hard, translucent and opaque, rest and motion.

For the beginner, the best way to see if a design will be appropriate for a rug is to copy and enlarge the design. It is very helpful to see the design's actual size. When you have the enlarged picture of the rug, use yarn, swatches of cloth, or articles of clothing to give you an idea of how the colors will look. If you are unsure of the design, look at it over a period of several days, from all angles, at night and during the day. If it turns out that the design is not right, you will see why and be able to choose another with more confidence. You can begin with a familiar picture, which guarantees its successful translation to the rug.

The complexities of line and shadow will be easier to duplicate when the design is enlarged to the size of the rug.

Most of the rugmakers represented in this book work from a scale drawing or sketch. Some of these drawings are included to give you an idea of how they look compared with the finished rug. A good exercise in rug sketching is to draw a rug shown in this book which

utilizes the same technique you plan to use.

Tile manufacturers use mirrors to show customers how a sample looks in a field of its kind. Using mirrors in this way also gives the rugmaker an excellent way to test how a figure, motif, or color combination looks when repeated on a large scale. Place four mirrors or mirror tiles at right angles to form a box, with the design as the floor of the box. Look down into the box to see the design repeated ad infinitum in the mirrors. If you want to see how a symmetrical design will look, place half the design at right angles to a mirror. A quarter of the design is repeated three times when it is placed on the floor between two mirrors at right angles. The latter method is often used in carpet showrooms to demonstrate samples of patterned carpets.

If you are copying a design, try to draw it freehand in order to familiarize yourself with it. If you don't know how to draw, first copy freehand the contours of the shapes. Follow the contours with your eye, moving your pencil along the paper at the same speed. (I suggest looking at the first lesson in *The Natural Way to Draw* by Kimon Nicolaïdes [Houghton Mifflin, 1941].) Don't lift your pencil from the paper or even look at the paper until you are finished with the drawing. The chances are that your drawing will be accurate, with everything in the right proportions. When you are drawing a line, imagine the line to be an outside edge of something. Push the pencil around in a way that makes all curves, outside curves; the result will be a fuller and more realistic drawing.

Try using different materials for drawing rug designs. Use crayons, watercolors, felt-tip pens, India ink, torn pieces of paper, chalk, stencils, or block prints. A crayon sketch on watercolor paper, or a paper with a coarse grain, is good for drawing hooked rug designs. Short strokes with a felt-tip marker or watercolors give an excellent idea of how a rya will look. Smudge the edges of the drawing slightly to resemble a cut pile, or use India ink over watercolors. If lighter colors are used first, others can be blended in.

Keep a notebook of possible rug designs and try to think of ideas for future projects.

Arrange shapes in rug designs so that they will be interesting to look at from different sides. You can do this by repeating a shape at other angles, enlarging it or superimposing other images on it. Draw backgrounds with a mixture of both light and dark shading. When you have chosen a design, consider the type of technique that is most suitable for it. Decide on the height of pile, the size of the rug, whether yarn or material will be used, and whether any colors need to be dyed. Your first choice of a rug design will be the hardest to make, but after the first rug you will be much more knowledgeable and confident about choosing your next design.

Color in Rugs

A summary of Western achievements in color theory can suggest to you some ways in which to best utilize color. Aristotle discovered that colors occurred between the extremes of black and white. Leonardo da Vinci realized that when the eye sees a pure color and immediately closes, an afterimage of the color's com-

Plate 3 "Ochre Spot" (38" × 61"), punch needle hooked by Marla Mallett.

plement is seen. For example, after red, the eye sees green, after blue it sees orange, after yellow it sees violet. In 1666 Isaac Newton, then twenty-three years old, experimented with a prism which broke up sunlight into six colors. A century later, Jacob Clebon used sheets of primary colors (red, yellow, and blue) and overlapped them to derive the six tertiary colors: yellow-orange, red-orange, red-violet, blue-violet, blue-green, and yellow-green.

In the nineteenth century, the German poet Goethe made very significant discoveries by performing experiments with color. He made a scale of the colors and gave each color a number based on its luminosity. He found that

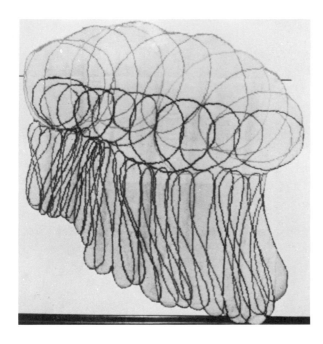

Figs. 2-3, 2-4 Latch hooked wall hangings by Traute Ishida.

yellow was the brightest color and gave it the number 3, orange received the number 4, red and green both rated 6, blue was 8, and purple was the darkest at 9. Based on this scale, Goethe arranged the colors proportionately so that each could attain its maximum vividness in relation to the others. For instance, the ratio of purple to yellow is 9:3. For the best effect the correct proportion would be three times more purple than yellow.

In 1835, Michel Chevreul returned to Leonardo da Vinci's discovery about pure color. Chevreul discovered that by putting a color next to its complement, the eye did not manufacture an afterimage. Sir David Brewster was responsible for returning to Isaac Newton's color prism. Colors are something to see; they do not exist in their own right. In absence of light there is no color. Edward E. Herring, a German psychologist, discovered that colors were pigmentary.

In the early twentieth century, Albert H. Munsell defined *hue* as shades of a color closely related, *value* as the light tone, and *chroma* as the intensity of a color. He devised a tree for the refinements of color and put white at the top and black at the roots.

Wilhelm Ostwald, in 1909, dissected the cornea of an eye to find that when light entered the eye, the mind fragmented the light into colors. Color, therefore, in order to exist, required a physical response.

Johannes Itten formulated a color theory which demonstrated, in part, that neutral gray was the ideal balance because there was no afterimage. When colors of the same light value are mixed, the result is a comparable gray. Gray can be considered a resting place for the eye.

Johannes Itten taught at the Bauhaus. His students learned about color without any dependence on form. His first assignment required students to paint colors in evenly spaced blocks so that the colors were confined to the same shape. This allowed the students to concentrate on color, not shape.

Complementary colors reach maximum brilliance when they are adjacent to each other: when yellow is placed next to violet, blue next to orange, and red next to green.

Gray near a color partially compensates for its complementary color because gray is the balance between the color and its complement. If a rug has both red and gray in it, the gray near the red will appear greenish. When blue dominates, the gray looks somewhat like orange, and the gray will look purplish if a yellow and gray rug is made. By extension, colors are brighter when next to any dark neutral area.

The eye automatically blends alternating stripes of color. For instance, if you hook alternating rows of red and green, the area will look brown from afar. Often rugmakers find this to be an effective means of introducing another color into the rug.

A carefully planned range of colors is much better than too many colors mixed together in the same rug. If there are too many colors, the eye will get tired looking at the rug; or the effect will be more of light and dark areas rather than many different colors. Consider the proportions of colors to each other, and if you want help in choosing a sample of colors, look at color combinations in wallpaper and especially in paintings. You will often find a delightful use of color.

Shades of a color are more distinct if they are separated by either black or white. Where there are several shades of a color too much alike, there will not be enough light-dark differentiation between them. The color in each shade will be reduced, thus making the colors muddy-looking.

Colors will stand out more on a contrasting background: dark colors against white backgrounds, and light colors on dark backgrounds. White often seems to expand when it is surrounded by a dark shade. Furthermore, white lightens colors when little dots of white are hooked or knotted through an area of a color. A bright lamp intensifies color in a rug.

Another contrast is between warm and cool colors. A test was devised to show to what degree a color contributes to the temperature of a room. Two rooms were painted, one in blue-green, a cool color, the other in red-orange, a warm color. In the blue-green room people felt cold at 59 degrees, but in the red-orange room people did not feel cold until the temperature was between 52 and 54 degrees. Colors warm a place by stimulating the circulation. Since a rug is inherently a soft, warm surface, you can capitalize on this feature by choosing warm colors for it.

Finally, an important fact to remember is that colors are brighter when the pile is cut because all the fibers of the yarn are exposed to the light. When the pile is left in loops, the colors are confined and therefore are dimmer.

Fig. 2-5 Untitled woven rya (3' × 5') by Jack Arends. There are two to four rows per inch and six to eight knots per inch, and the pile is ½ inch to 2 inches. It took him "approximately forty minutes per row."

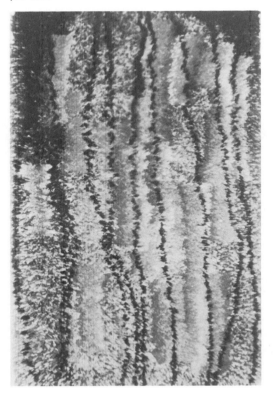

Plate 4 (*above*)   Latch hooked wall hanging by Traute Ishida.

Plate 5   Latch hooked rug designed by Louisa Calder.

Plate 6 Detail of unicorn, "The Beginning of the Beginning." (See Fig. 8-12, page 66.)

3

Duplicating, Enlarging, and Transferring Designs

Practically every rug originates as a small picture that has been enlarged to suit the rug. A design taken directly from a large painting or mural is modified by the medium. Because it's a rug, the texture and the angle of perception will be considerably different from that of the work it is copied from.

Most experienced rugmakers are able to make a rug that looks exactly as they had visualized it. You will be able to achieve this in time, but for now you will need to know the best methods of duplicating pictures for your first few rugs.

Hand hook, rya, and latch hook designs are transferred to the front side of the canvas, while speed hooked rugs are worked from the back to the front. All designs except symmetrical speed hooked designs are transferred face down onto the rug backing. The design can be copied face down and this copy can be enlarged and transferred to the backing.

The clearest tracing of a picture can be made by taping together the tracing paper and the picture and holding them against a window on a bright day or by tracing on the illuminated surface of a light table. If the original design is in a book, be sure to put masking tape along one side of the tracing so you can fold the tracing back and compare it with the original, to check for lines that might otherwise be lost. A pencil tracing cannot pick up the texture because the shadings that lend depth to the picture are too light to trace. The texture often asserts the necessary feeling of space, and without this the tracing often looks flat and discordant. The first thing to consider is that in the enlarged version the shading and details will be easier to reproduce. Secondly, the colors of the yarn and the height of pile can replace much of the tonal qualities of the original. Many pictures are even improved.

Another way to copy a picture is to trace it directly with crayons or felt-tip pens, using the light colors first and blending in the darker shades afterward. This is faster, easier, and more appropriate for many pictures.

Xeroxing is a useful method for testing various color combinations. Xerox several copies of your design and freely experiment with color. If a photoduplicating machine is not available, trace the picture and try color combinations in different parts of a sketch before coloring the whole picture.

Graph paper is excellent for both scale drawings and geometric designs. Isometric graph paper, which is for drawing in perspective, is sold at drafting supply stores. All the lines on this paper cross at a 60-degree angle.

It's a good idea to enlarge and transfer the pattern to the backing at the same time. Use washable crayons, chalk, or charcoal—anything that can be erased in the event that you change your mind about the design. (Both monk's cloth and burlap will stretch when attached to a frame, but monk's cloth will stretch

Fig. 3-1 Scale drawing of latch hooked wall hanging designed by Marcel Breuer for Torin Inc., Torrington, Conn.

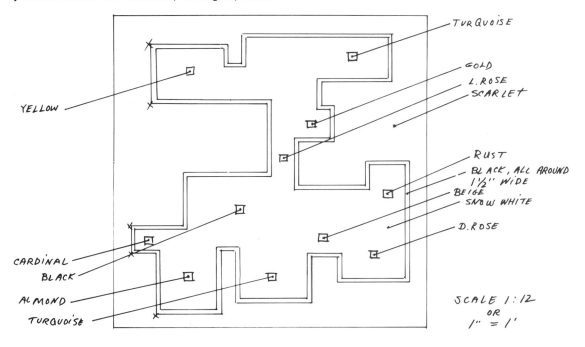

more, at least one inch on each side.) Center the design on the backing; don't have the borders too near the edge of the cloth. If a frame side is two inches wide, estimate five inches from the border of the pattern to the edge of the monk's cloth, or three inches if burlap is used.

Ryas are generally not made from a design drawn on the backing, but rather from a graph paper chart in which every square represents a rya knot. To give a more accurate illustration of the rya pile, two vertical squares for each rya knot can be used to depict the long pile. The design can of course be drawn on the backing cloth, but this is seldom done because a rya has no details that require exact reproduction.

Paper must be put under the latch hook mesh backing to prevent ink from going through when the design is transferred. It is best to draw the design on the paper and trace through the holes of the canvas. Draw the design so that the lines cover the latch hook holes completely. Do not draw some lines along just one thread of the mesh.

Whichever method you use, choose an indelible marker to finalize the drawing on the rug canvas or fabric backing.

Enlarging and Transferring Designs

A pantograph is an instrument for enlarging designs from one and a half to eight times their original size, and for reducing designs in these same proportions. One arm has a tracer point that follows the lines of the design, while the other arm copies the design in a different size. It is a valuable instrument for enlarging small pictures, or portions of a design, to a size that is convenient for transferring to the backing. Pantographs are available in art supply stores and range in price from four dollars to fourteen dollars, depending upon quality.

Overhead projectors (also called opaque or positive projectors) are the quickest and easi-

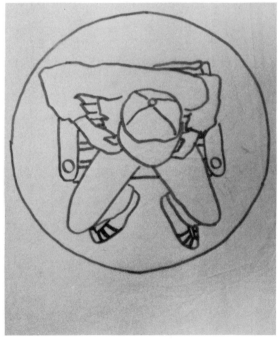

Fig. 3-2 Two tracings for "Flicka's Rug": one for color (*top*), the other for outline.

Fig. 3-3 "Flicka's Rug," finished. Designed by Flicka Leibert, this rug was hooked in a 1-inch pile by the author.

est method for enlarging and transferring a design. They are able to magnify to a size that is equal to the needs of any rugmaker. The size of the image can be adjusted contingent upon the distance between the backing material and the projector. A projector is very expensive and therefore probably not accessible to many lay rugmakers. Almost every school has at least one of these projectors because of their usefulness in enlarging materials from books and other sources for special teaching effects. If you can persuade a teacher to let you use one in a classroom after school, then do try this method.

A slide projector can also be helpful to the rugmaker. First photograph the design. Then use a slide projector to project the slide onto the backing material that you have tacked to the wall. Focus and then transfer.

The grid method is the most common method for enlarging designs. A scale drawing is made (fig. 3–7). As the scale is enlarged the design will be correctly enlarged. If you want to use this method to transfer the design to a backing that has marker threads, make the small scale according to these markers. Usually cotton rug backing is apportioned along 3-inch lines and mesh in 3-inch squares.

To make the grid, first fold or mark the design into even parts. Diagonals are especially good, but squares are more often used. A round design can be folded into pie slices. Ovals and elliptical shapes should be framed in the closest conventional shape. Folded or marked, the design is now on a scale for the rug. The next step is to divide the backing into the same number of spaces (squares, pie shapes, etc.) as on the design.

If you have divided the design into squares press the sharp point of a pencil into the backing cloth and pull straight across the weave. The line will more realistically reflect the weave of the cloth. Later, these lines will also serve as an indicator of the straightness of the backing cloth.

If you have divided the design into pie shapes using diagonal lines, put the sketch in the corner of the backing cloth and follow the diagonal lines across the cloth. If the design is complicated, put the sketch in the adjacent corner and follow the lines across to bisect.

When the design is fully enlarged, go over all the lines with an indelible marker so that every line meets and the whole picture stands out clearly.

Sketches and photographs can be blown up to poster size by sending them to a mail order company or by taking them to a local photographer. The usual offer extends to both negatives and positives and the common size is 2 feet by 3 feet, or poster size. Before having a design for a speed hooked rug blown up, flip the design over, trace it, and have this blown up. Art supply stores sell large sheets of carbon paper that are useful for transferring posters and large designs. Put the backing on the floor, place the carbon paper on the backing with the ink side facing down, and put the large design or poster on top. With a blunt pencil or a perforating wheel, mark the lines of the design. Go over these lines immediately with an indelible pen.

A stencil is good for a pattern you might want to repeat or for a poster you don't want

Clockwise from above:

Fig. 3-4   A painting by Fletcher Copp being traced onto loose woven burlap.

Fig. 3-5   The materials needed to reproduce Fletcher Copp's painting—yarn, dyes, burlap backing, and frame.

Fig. 3-6   To figure out how much yarn of each color is needed in a rug, first draw a sketch of the design on draft paper.

Fig. 3-7   Scale drawing is useful for enlarging designs and color coding.

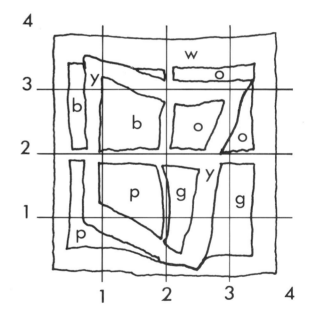

Rug dimension: 2′ × 2′ = 16 boxes

white	4 squares = 4/16 or 1/4 rug
blue	2 squares = 2/16 or 1/8 rug
orange	2 squares = 2/16 or 1/8 rug
green	2 squares = 2/16 or 1/8 rug
yellow	4 squares = 4/16 or 1/4 rug
purple	2 squares = 2/16 or 1/8 rug

to trace. Enlarge the pattern and/or paste the poster to oaktag and cut the shapes out with a mat knife or good sharp scissors. Be careful where you cut the stencil. Several layers of newspapers make the best surface for cutting.

The old-fashioned method of ironing a design to transfer it to the backing has been improved because of a special ink transfer pencil. One application can make several transfers from one drawing. Trace the drawing onto light paper and iron the back side of the paper over the rug backing. The design will be transferred in reverse, perfect for speed hookers. In doing a hand hooked rug (not speed hooked), you could trace the back side of the design and iron this to the backing. The picture now faces right side up. This method is only suitable for cloth, not canvas backing.

Burlap sacks often have interesting designs on them which can be speed hooked exactly as they appear by putting pins through the fabric along the lines of the design. Spread the opened burlap bag out in front of a well-lit window and draw the lines between the pins on the burlap back. This method could also be utilized when a design has been mistakenly put on the wrong side of the backing. Or, you could speed hook through the design for the picture in reverse.

Many stationery stores sell stencils of numbers and letters in several sizes that can be used in rugmaking. A name, date, or inscription adds a very personal touch to a rug. But if you write something, make sure the letters and numbers are positioned correctly, depending on the type of rug hook you are employing. To put letters or numbers on a speed hooked rug, first draw the figures on a piece of paper. Hold the paper up to a light source; the lettering should face the light. What you see will be the lettering reversed. This reverse image can now be used as a guide or duplicated on the wrong side of the backing to assure proper spacing and position.

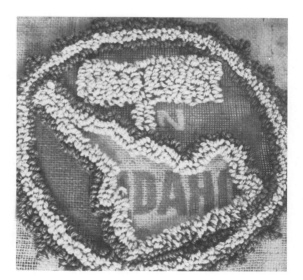

Fig. 3-8 (*left*) "Grown in Idaho," burlap sack to be hooked by Michel Little.

Fig. 3-9 Partially hooked pillow, made with a speed tufting tool.

Fig. 3-10   Later progress on Michel Little's pillow.

Fig. 3-11   Back view of completed pillow.

Fig. 3-12   Finished pillow, "Grown in Idaho" by Michel Little.

Color Coding

Color coding is necessary if you want to determine exactly how much yarn of each color is needed in your rug. Return to the scale drawing (fig. 3-7). Give a number to each color and mark each box of the scale drawing with the appropriate number. If there are two colors in a space, write the number for the dominant color, or, if they are equal, one half to each. Determine the amount of yarn or material required by counting the number of boxes of each color. Put this number over the total number of boxes to complete the fraction of specific color in the rug. For instance, if you have sixteen boxes, with four boxes of white, then $\frac{4}{16}$ or $\frac{1}{4}$ of the rug will be white. If the rug is 4 square feet at $\frac{1}{4}$-inch pile, about one pound of yarn is required.

Fig. 3-13 Sketch of a rug designed by architect John Johansen for Rufus and Leslie Stillman in 1966. The sketch was painted on palette paper and the background textured by pulling a shingle through the paint.

Plate 7 Finished rug.

4

Introduction to Rug Hooking

Rug hooking, that is, covering a piece of cloth with hundreds of loops of material, originated with the eighteenth-century English weavers. The weavers were allowed to keep the remnants of cloth and bits of yarn not used by the looms. These discards were randomly hooked through a foundation material to make hearth mats. But since the loops were loose and hooked far apart, a mat could not be expected to last more than a year.

Colonial sailors also took to this spare-time occupation. During their voyages they hooked wool pictures, which were probably used as pillows or covers of some sort. Their work was enthusiastically received and copied in early America.

Only the very rich in America had carpets imported from France or England. Most people, if they had anything on their floors, put down painted sailcloth "floor cloths," which were copied from European tile designs. Such floor cloths were not very durable, so people turned to hooked rugs and developed techniques to make suitable floor covers. Women tore up old clothes into strips and hooked the strips through a gunnysack until the sack was covered and could be put on the floor. Rugs that were loosely hooked fell apart, those with an even pile in tight rows were heavier, warmer, and lasted longer. Sometimes the loops were pulled high and clipped if the rug became too faded or dirty. But most of the rugs were hooked with a low even pile from 1/8 inch to 1/4 inch high.

The better a rug was made, the longer it took for the rugmaker to hook it. One square foot of a rug might take between four and five hours to complete. In addition, preparation work had to be done. Each square foot required at least four square feet of material that had to be washed and then torn into strips after the seams were ripped out.

Hooked rugs helped to keep heat in a room because they covered drafty floorboards. They also solved the problem of what to do with worn-out clothes and provided a useful and relaxing pastime for the long evenings at a time when there were few diversions. In those days newspapers were at best weekly, except in large cities, and of course radio, television, and movies did not exist.

The designs of the early hooked rugs were simple. Color came from the clothes and other materials used, or from natural dyes. Since most clothes were black, dark green, or gray, there were few rugs with bright colors.

Rug hooking was a well-established craft by the time of the Civil War. The first real boom, however, occurred right after the war when Maine veteran E. S. Frost began printing rug patterns with a zinc stencil on burlap. The rug patterns elevated the art of rug hooking and renewed enthusiasm. Rugs became sources of artistic decoration. Commercial patterns solved the problem that faced most rug hookers— which was large areas of hooking on nothing

Fig. 4-1 "Clematis" pattern for hooked rug, available from Heirloom Rugs.

but a crude design of their own with limited choice of color. In subsequent years rug patterns proliferated, and a large quantity of small low-pile rugs filled with flowers, scrolls, landscapes, and geometric shapes began to be turned out in homes all over America. These were considered the most suitable designs for the many hours of rug hooking involved, and reflected the fashions and interests of the times.

Chemical dyes were introduced at just about the same time as rug patterns. So it is not surprising that shading became an important aspect of rug design. According to Barbara Zarbock in *The Complete Book of Rug Hooking,* at times the shading in very small figures was so intricate that it was difficult, if not impossible, for a person looking down at the rug to distinguish the color gradations and fine details. Thus the desired effect was lost. In the 1890s, hooked rugs, along with other Victorian "dust ketchers," were put away in attics.

The introduction of special rug yarn, modern techniques of visual reproduction, and speed hooks have created new possibilities for rug hookers. What used to take four hours to complete can now be done in one hour or less. There are also many speed hooking tools available that allow for varying heights of pile, textural variations, and personal preferences. These tools—the punch needle, the shuttle hook, and the speed tufter—are discussed at length in the following chapters.

Fig. 4-2 Pattern for hooked rug from Wilson Brothers, manufacturers of the Tru-Gyde shuttle hook.

Rug yarn is thick and comes in almost every color imaginable. The yarn comes in skeins, which eliminates the preparation time that was previously necessary when hooking materials had to be first cut or torn. Unlike flat material that was folded and hooked, rug yarn is round and can be hooked with greater variation. It is easier to hook a much higher pile with rug yarn.

Sources of inspiration for designs are more accessible today, and modern duplicating methods make it a pleasure to enlarge and transfer designs for rug patterns.

The interest in and regard for crafts has

been an important influence on many people. Now that people no longer *have* to make rugs for their homes, the modern rugmaker can be creative about rugmaking rather than primarily utilitarian.

Rug patterns are still popular. Both traditional and contemporary patterns are available through a number of outlets. The prices are reasonable (usually less than fifty cents a square foot) but will vary depending on the design and size. Most patterns are printed on burlap, but some are available on monk's cloth for speed hookers. If you are planning to hook an Oriental design, or a complex floral pattern, or you simply do not want to design your own, it makes sense to buy a pattern. You can still, of course, add details of your own.

General Rules of Rug Hooking

A hooked rug can look the same whether a hand hook or a speed hook is used except that a speed hooked rug always has an even pile. With a hand hook the height of the pile can vary because each loop is pulled up individually. Also the spacing is controlled completely by the hand hooker, whereas speed hooks often have a device to space the loops automatically.

The French tapestry maker Jean Lurçat described the texture of his work as "gooseflesh," and the same applies even more so to hooked loops. The low pile looks grainy and the direction of the loops is very obvious. The higher the pile, however, the wider the loops spread apart and the harder it is to distinguish the direction in which they were hooked.

There are three variations in texture that can be utilized:

1. The loops can be split open with scissors for an even tufted surface. The pile has to be at least ⅜ inch high so that it will keep its place in the weave of the cloth. It is easier to do the cutting by rows while the rug is being made, although the loops can

be cut afterward with narrow-blade scissors.

2. The tops of the loops can be sheared for a velvety pile. At least a ⅜-inch pile should be left standing. It is easier to shear the rug when it is finished and the backing is latexed so that no loops can be pulled out inadvertently. Bent shears or sheep shears can be employed for this effect.

3. The loops can be partially cut so that the rug has a combination of cut and uncut pile.

Rug hooking can be done in any direction. The direction in which you loop affects the appearance of the rug. The direction of the uncut pile is emphasized when it is hooked in long straight lines, horizontally, vertically, diagonally, or in definite patterns like zigzags or spirals. Lower uncut pile yields more clarity of line direction. Cut pile has no distinguishable direction at all.

An easy way to hook is to follow the contours of the shapes, or if you want to design the texture of the rug before hooking it, draw the direction of the pile with a pencil or fine-line marker. If you want to minimize the texture of the loops, hook the yarn or material in short wavy lines that go in all directions.

Separate shapes by at least ¾ inch. When two sections of pile higher than ½ inch are hooked next to each other, the loops will interlock and give the edge a jagged look. The higher the pile, the more noticeable the edge. If you want to have a hard edge along each part, hook a row with a shorter pile between the two sections. The dividing row should be half the height of the rest of the pile so that it cannot be seen but is able to separate the two areas on either side of it. If you want the sections even more distinctly apart, hook the row slightly higher or hook two rows between them.

When you wish to accent one spot, use a slightly longer loop at that point so that it will be clearly visible. (See fig. 4-5.)

Ends of yarn and material must be poked through to the pile side so that a row will not be pulled out accidentally. The rug hooker should do this whenever a row is begun or

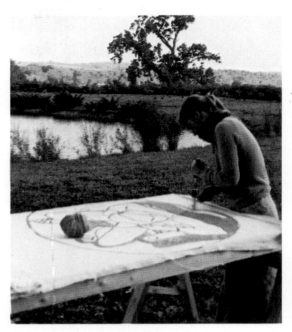

Plate 8 Author hooking with a speed tufting tool on a George Wells–designed horizontal frame.

Plate 9 Latch hooked wall hanging by Traute Ishida.

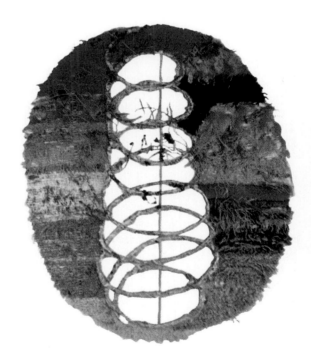

Fig. 4-3 Navaho rug pattern for hooked rug design from Wilson Brothers.

follow. This area can be rehooked easily. If the loops have been split or sheared, they have to be removed individually. Once the rug has been latexed, the loops are sealed to the backing and no more changes in the pile can be made. A hooked rug really must be latexed or else the loops will be pulled out by shoes and pets. If you think that you might want to change the color or design of part of a wall hanging, do not latex that part of the backing.

A hooked rug may have as many as thirty loops per square inch, which affords the rug-maker the opportunity to make fine details. A hooked rug has the densest pile of any of the rugs described in this book. The loops must be spaced correctly. If there are too many loops, the rug will buckle and not lie flat. If there are too few loops, the backing will show from the pile side.

Table 3
The Spacing of Loops

low pile ¼–½ in.	30 per sq. in.	5 loops, 6 rows
med. pile ½–1 in.	24–25 per sq. in.	4 loops, 6 rows
		5 loops, 5 rows
high pile 1–2 in.	20 per sq. in.	4 loops, 5 rows

In order to space the loops correctly, the yarn or material must be kept slack. If your loops are uneven, it is probably because not enough yarn is being fed to the hook. If there is enough yarn, then the problem is either that the backing is not tight enough on the frame or the hook is not being held correctly. Skeins and balls of yarn have a tendency to fall off the frame when the yarn is pulled. To avoid this, keep the yarn in a basket or bag by your feet.

When a figure is hooked in one color, it appears flat. But you can hook a figure so that it looks three dimensional. This illusion is produced by dividing the figure into a front, middle, and back. Hook the front part in a light color, the middle in a darker color, and the back part in an even deeper color. This method of highlighting is a very effective and simple way to make your rug look more realistic and interesting.

ended, or at the end of a section. (See figs. 4-6 and 4-7.)

A crossover is something to be avoided. It is an extra layer of material that can be easily pulled out and the row of loops with it. It occurs when you hook over the back of a loop in order to get to an unhooked section.

Because rows of uncut pile are easy to pull out, changes can be made whenever the need arises. From either the back or the front of the rug, pull one of the loops and the rest will

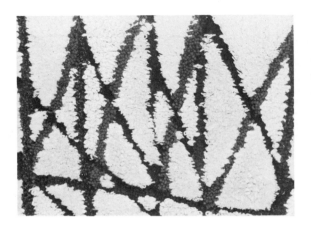

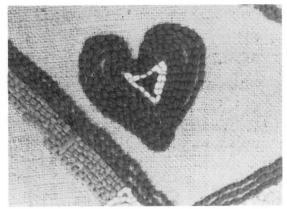

Clockwise from above:

Fig. 4-4 Detail from "Brown Furrows" (45″ × 70″), wall hanging hooked with a punch needle and wool yarn and strips by Marla Mallett.

Fig. 4-5 To accent a feature, hook it with a higher pile.

Fig. 4-6 To keep a row from being pulled out accidentally, ends must be cut off short and pushed through to the pile side right away. They can also be cut off tall so they are easy to see and, later, when the rug is finished they can be cut short and pushed through.

Fig. 4-7 Pile side of "Mermaid with Parakeet" by Matisse, showing a cut-off end.

5

Rug Hooking Equipment

Rug Yarn

Wool fleece is soft and durable and, best of all, it has great resiliency. It springs back after it has been walked on or crushed. Fleece from different breeds of sheep is blended so that various strengths and weights of wool yarn can be produced. The usual width of a strand of wool rug yarn is $3/16$ inch, and comes in 4, 5, or 6 ply. Wool has some other advantages too. Because it is opaque, it can be dyed very successfully, and even colored wool yarn does not show dirt easily.

Wool rug yarn, however, may soon become the exclusive luxury of home crafters and of those who buy custom-made rugs. This is because of the increased use of synthetic fibers in commercial carpeting. Wool was surpassed by nylon in commercial rug construction in

1964. Synthetic fibers are much cheaper to manufacture than wool yarn. Before wool yarn is even made the fleece first has to be sheared from the sheep and then washed and spun. But the real reason that synthetic fibers have been developed so extensively over the last few years is that they can withstand the wear and tear caused by modern carpet-making machinery. Synthetics were the end product of a search for a more usable material, not necessarily a better one. Luckily, wool is still found in great abundance and is still widely used in clothing. Rug yarns are available from Argentina, Canada, New Zealand, the Near East, and Scandinavia. Mainland China was formerly a very large supplier of rug yarn to the United States and because of new trade agreements it may be again.

Rug yarn is sold in four- or eight-ounce skeins. Usually it is sold as loose skeins, which means it is one piece of yarn wrapped into an oval and then twisted like a pastry loaf. Sometimes rug yarn is sold in pull skeins like knitting yarn. Pull skeins are wound so that a piece of yarn is pulled from either the center of the skein or from around its outside edge. The advantage of a pull skein is that the yarn is ready to hook, and also, it cannot tangle. It only takes a few minutes, however, to wind a loose skein into a ball or cut it into strips before hooking.

If you use imported yarn, you are obliged to pay a 15 percent duty. Despite the extra expense, foreign rug yarn is often cheaper than domestic. Prices range from as low as $2.50 to as high as $12.00 per pound. However, good Canadian yarns can be had for $3.50 including duty, whereas domestic yarns of the same quality are generally $4.00 to $5.00. The most expensive rug yarns are available in many colors and usually feel nicer because the wool is of the very best quality and is better prepared. Obviously, part of the greater cost is the expertise in dyeing. With large orders of at least twenty pounds suppliers give a substantial discount. Undyed yarn in natural white and grays can usually be bought for less than dyed yarn.

There are many advantages to using synthetic yarns in rugmaking. First of all, synthetic fibers are to some degree translucent, which means that the colors are bright and the fibers are shinier than those of wool. Second, synthetic yarns are lighter than wool so you are buying more yards per pound. Often synthetic yarns are thinner than wool so that several different-colored strands can be used together. Third, because synthetic fibers absorb a minimum of moisture, they dry quickly after they have been washed. Fourth, the colors never fade. Fifth, the manufacturers try to make them feel as soft as wool.

The following are some synthetic yarns that are of interest to the home rugmaker.

1. *Acrylics.* They are soft and have good texture retention and resiliency. Modacrylics feel even more like wool but are not as resilient as acrylic yarn.
2. *Nylon.* It is unsurpassed in its resistance to abrasion, but it is coarse-feeling. Half nylon/half wool is a very good combination.
3. *Polyester.* It is easy to maintain and feels good to the touch, but its resiliency is not admirable. Because of its molecular structure, it is very hard to dye. This accounts for its late entrance on the market.

As indicated in Table 4 below, buying blends of wool and synthetic yarns gives the rugmaker the advantage of buying more yards to the pound because of the lightness of synthetics. About a half-pound of wool rug yarn will cover a square foot of a rug 1 inch high; three strands of synthetic yarn will cover the same area.

Table 4

	3/16 in. 100% wool	3/16 in. 1/2 wool-1/2 nylon	2 ply, 1/16 in. synthetic (3 strands together)
4 oz. (1/4 lb.)	80 yds.	140 yds.	240 yds.
8 oz. (1/2 lb.)	160 yds.	280 yds.	480 yds.
12 oz. (3/4 lb.)	240 yds.	420 yds.	720 yds.
16 oz. (1 lb.)	320 yds.	560 yds.	960 yds.

Material for Rug Hooking

Any old clothes, and especially coats and blankets, can be utilized in hooking rugs. "Little Boy's Toys" by Anna Sunnergren (color plate 10) is an example of a rug made with recycled materials. Much of the material was collected in secondhand stores. The colors of the rug are khaki, beige, and burnt sienna. The colors were easy to find and are particularly suitable to the subject matter of the rug. In some areas of the rug the hooking has been reversed so that you see the back of the loops and not the pile.

Shuttle hooks and hand hooks are the best tools to use with material because fabric tends to break or its edges catch in speed hooks. Some rugmakers have successfully hooked materials with a punch needle, but for the beginner the best tools are those I have mentioned. Shuttle hooks and hand hooks do not have shafts that the fabric could get stuck in.

Usually material is hooked in a low uncut pile because of its thinness and flatness. Even when cloth is folded—and strips wider than ⅜ inch must have their edges folded under so the loops look right—it doesn't have enough resiliency to be hooked into a high pile.

It is difficult to determine by weight how much material will cover a particular area. Light and heavy materials can be used together in a rug, but the lighter material must be cut into wider strips to insure that the density of the pile remains well balanced. An easy way to test how much material is needed is to lay four layers of the material over the area to be hooked. If you cannot find enough material of one color for a particular section, select enough material from closely related shades to cover it. Hook some of each shade in each part of the section.

Pick materials that can all be cleaned in the same way and wash them all to check colorfastness. If you use a washing machine and hot water, the fabric will mat. This is desirable because with a tight weave the edges will not fray as much when the material is cut into strips for hooking.

Any material can be used, but it should be tested first to see how it looks hooked and to determine how easy it is to work with. Wool is the most popular material. Silk and velvet are both recommended because of their fine qualities. (Black velvet is also the blackest black available in a fabric.) Cotton gets dirty easily, and the loops do not spread out and cover any area beyond that which is actually made into a loop.

Table 5 on page 62 lists fabrics and the thicknesses of strips to be hooked, and also gives the area that one square yard of each fabric covers.

Foundation Materials

Burlap is the traditional rug backing material for hooked rugs. Burlap is cheap, costing approximately eight to sixteen cents a square foot. To its disadvantage is the fact that it is made of jute, a vegetable fiber. Consequently, burlap does not stretch well and the threads can eventually dry out and crack.

Most antique hooked rugs owe their longevity to the fact that the edges were not hemmed but bound. A rug with a tightly folded hem is more likely to dry out before a rug that has a binding, which reinforces the edges and eases the strain. Another reason many hooked rugs from the last century have lasted is that they were hooked in a very low pile with thin strips of material on double-ply gunnysacks. This method of hooking causes less strain on the burlap. Burlap sacks are still recommended, but check them for worn spots and patch any holes before you use them. For most of the hooked rugs made today, there is a single-ply burlap in a 10- or 12-ounce weight. It has an even weave with practically no knots to impede the progress of the rug hook, and it comes in widths of 40, 48, and 60 inches.*

* See list of suppliers on pages 133–134.

Plate 10 "Little Boy's Toys" (4' × 5'), a shuttle hooked rug made from wool strips by Anna Sunnergren.

Fig. 5-1 Pencil sketch by Anna Sunnergren's son, age five, from which "Little Boy's Toys" was designed.

To strengthen burlap, a latex finish is added to the backing after the rug is made. This seals the loops in place, and it also serves to keep the backing together, thus extending the rug's life.

Cotton is stronger and more elastic than burlap, and it is possible to stretch cotton tightly over a rug frame. For these reasons most rug hookers who use speed hooks prefer a cotton backing. Cotton is available in soft weaves and comes in many sizes.

The most popular cotton backing is called monk's cloth. It has a 2-ply weave that is strong enough to withstand penetration by a speed hook. Monk's cloth comes in widths of up to fifteen feet and often comes with colored marking threads woven in to make design computations easier. Monk's cloth costs about twenty cents a square foot.

Rug warp is the strongest cotton backing. It will permanently hold the closest packed and/or highest pile possible. It is sold by the yard and comes in widths of 28, 56, and 72 inches. It costs about fifty cents a square foot.

Any woven cloth can be used as a backing for rugs, but check it first by pushing the hook up and down through it. If the hook is easy to maneuver and you consider the cloth strong enough to hold the weight of the pile, then the cloth can probably be used successfully as a backing. Loose and thin weaves are better suited to wall hangings and pillows than rugs.

Frames

The purpose of the rug frame is to hold the backing material taut. This permits the rug-maker to hook consistently evenly and quickly. Although hand hooking can be done without a frame (see Chapter 6), a frame is essential for all speed hooking projects. The large frames, vertical and horizontal, are easy to make yourself. A large rug can be made on a small frame by hooking the rug in sections and joining them afterward, but it is often easier to do the rug in one piece at one time.

A canvas stretcher or wooden picture frame can be used as a small hooking frame. If it is wobbly, reinforce it with metal braces inside the corners. Prepare for hooking by propping the frame against a window ledge, table, or chair, or attach legs to the corners so that the hook can go under the cloth without jabbing you accidentally.

The Emkay wooden frame from Braid Aid is designed to hold a hooking area of approximately one square foot. A tray is placed under the frame for storing equipment. The cost of this frame is thirteen dollars. Braid Aid also sells round hoop and oval frames that are of no use to speed hookers because they are too delicate, but they are used by many hand hookers. The round hoops have either a 14- or a 23-inch diameter; the 14-inch one has a stand that can be purchased separately. The oval frame is 18 by 27 inches. The Puritan Lap frame, also sold by Braid Aid, is 12 by 16 inches and has metal points around the edges that secure the material. This feature has made it a popular frame.

The most popular frame is the Fraser Adjustable Rug Hooking Frame. It has standard size 40-inch crossbars, but there are also 20-, 30-, 50-, and 60-inch bars available to enable you to make any size rug. This is an easel frame: the top can be tilted to any angle and can be revolved completely to show the rug's other side. The cost of the frame is under twenty dollars.

It's not always necessary to buy frames; you may be able to improvise. For example, a wonderful frame for a square rug or a wall hanging is a folding card table with its top cut out. An old door without the screen or glass center can be placed on top of sawhorses or leaned against a wall to make a basic speed hooking frame. If, however, you want to make a frame, directions for both vertical and horizontal frames are given on pages 36–38.

Speed hooks are usually held at right angles to the material being hooked, but the frame can be at any angle that is most comfortable for the rugmaker. Each person will choose a frame best suited to his needs, but here are some general considerations to keep in mind:

1. The easel frame is small, portable, and can be easily adjusted to any height or angle. Also, extra backing can be rolled around the beams of the frame.
2. The vertical frame takes up less living space and is good for group projects. The backing is hemmed and laced to the frame, which means that when it is all hooked, the work is all done. Furthermore, the frame can be knocked down for storage.
3. The horizontal frame is ideal for stretching and keeping material taut with carpet stripping. The frame can have a moveable crossbar for different-size projects and extra ma-

Fig. 5-2 (*above*) Michel Little's vertical frame with stretched burlap backing.

Fig. 5-3 To stretch backing material evenly on a horizontal frame, start on one side and, if possible, follow a marker thread to keep backing even.

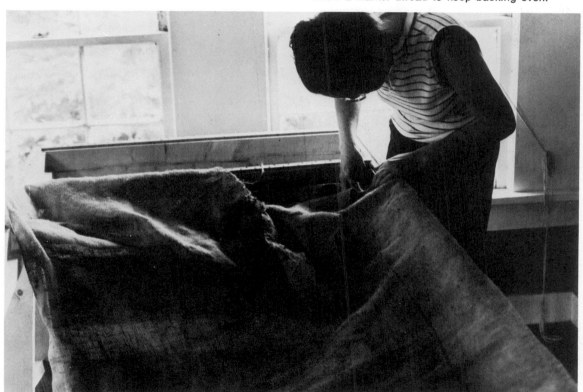

Fig. 5-4 Over tackless stripping pull the burlap or cotton up and over the tacks, as is illustrated here.

terial can extend from the sides. However, the rug has to be hemmed after it is hooked.

Directions for Making Rug Frames

For a vertical frame, buy four 1- by 2-inch boards and bolt the corners (or use C clamps). Install the frame on "platform feet" and add an angled support in the back to make the frame freestanding.

To make a horizontal frame, follow these instructions from George Wells, an extremely prolific rugmaker. Have four 2-by-4s cut to the length you want. The side pieces should not be more than 3 feet, otherwise you will not be able to reach the center of the rug. Nail or glue the frame together and add angle braces to the bottom to insure its strength. Nail two 2-by-2s along the inside lengths of the frame, even with the bottom of the frame. Cut a 2-by-2 as long as the inside width of the frame and lay it across so that it rests on the inserted 2-by-2s. This 2-by-2 is the crosspiece that enables you to adjust the length of a project. Screw corner braces to both ends of the crosspiece, and hammer roofing nails through the brace into the frame to keep the crosspiece in the desired position while speed hooking. For stability, the frame can lie on top of two sawhorses. Drive four nails into the sawhorses at the edges of the frame to hold it firmly.

Fastening the material to the frame requires some attention. There are two ways to do this, either by lacing or tacking. Some rugmakers prefer a combination of the two.

To lace, a cord or shoelace should be pushed through the backing, wrapped around the beam of the frame, and pushed back through the hem of the backing. It should then be tied off. This procedure should be followed completely around the frame every few inches. The lacing must be pulled tightly so that every side is equally stretched. If the size of the frame makes this procedure difficult, try one of the following variations.

If the backing is larger than the frame, roll the excess backing around parallel sides of the frame before lacing the backing taut. After this first section has been hooked, remove the lacing and pull the remaining backing across the frame—replace and proceed hooking. This is essentially the same as the standard lacing method, but the extra backing is wrapped around the frame so that it doesn't get in your way.

The following method is slightly more complicated to initiate, but once established is easier, especially if you are hooking a small rug and you do not have an adjustable frame. Take a piece of sailcloth or other heavy canvas and sew curtain rings along two parallel edges. Fold the sailcloth over a side of the frame so that you can lace the backing to the rings.

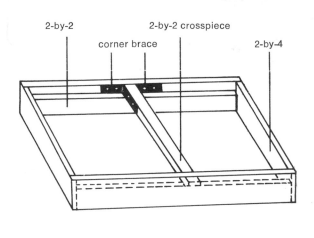

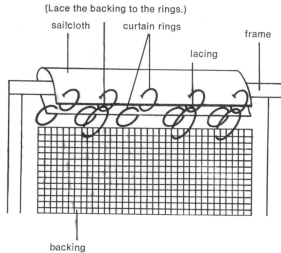

(Lace the backing to the rings.)

Fig. 5-5   Horizontal frame.

Fig. 5-6   Method 2: Fastening backing material to frame.

Fig. 5-7   Matisse rug with a George Wells horizontal frame.

Repeat this procedure for the other three sides. The backing, laced through the rings on all four sides, is now pulled tight. This method eliminates the necessity of having the backing itself laced directly to the beams.

It is easier to stretch a rug over carpet stripping if you get the help of two people. Carpet stripping is sold in carpet stores in 4-foot lengths and costs about four cents a foot. The strip has a double row of upward slanted tacks that are held between two layers of thin wood. The strip is nailed to the frame with the tacks pointing outward. First lay the material over the tacks on one side, then pull the backing on the frame's opposite side over the strips. Follow the same procedure for the other sides. The tacks will hold the backing perfectly.

Begin on one side of the frame and pull the backing evenly so that there is at least 4 inches, preferably more, between the rug pattern and the inside edge of the frame. It is better to have more space because monk's cloth can stretch up to 2 inches horizontally and vertically. If the pattern is too close to the frame, the speed hook won't be able to work. Move around the frame and pull the backing so that it is tight and the weave of the cloth is even. If it is unavoidable that the pattern edges get too close to the frame, pull the pattern so that at least one side can be completely hooked before rearranging the backing to work on another side. If there is excess material, roll it up as best you can or simply tuck it under the frame.

Carpet tacking is used by wall-to-wall carpeting installers. The tacks are very sharp and do a very good job. You may protect your arms from the tacks by placing a piece of foam rubber over the strips.

If you don't want to use carpet strips, nail individual carpet tacks through the material into the frame.

Hooks and other needles, punches, and tools are fully discussed in the following chapters. (See the Table of Contents.)

Fig. 5-8 Rug hooks (*left to right*): speed tufting tool, Susan Burr shuttlehook, Columbia Minerva deluxe punch needle.

Other Equipment (Material Cutters, Latex, Scissors)

A material cutter costs at least twenty dollars, but it is an invaluable device if you plan to cut any quantity of material. Several models, including some which clamp onto a table, are available with a choice of blades: #3 cuts six strips $3/32$ inch wide, #4 cuts four strips $1/8$ inch wide, #5 cuts three strips $5/32$ inch wide, #6 cuts three strips $3/16$ inch wide, and #8 cuts two strips $1/4$ inch wide. The alternatives to buying a material cutter are to tear the material or cut it into strips with scissors. These are two very time-consuming methods.

Latex is sold by the pint, quart, and gallon. A quart covers 9 square feet. It is applied to the back of a rug to seal the loops and make it skidproof. Sears, Roebuck sells Saf-T-Bak, an especially popular brand with rugmakers. Another brand, Griptex, is sold in hardware stores. The side of the can is the "applicator," but I recommend using a putty knife or paint brush to distribute the latex. Hardware stores often carry a latex that can be sprayed on.

A small pair of scissors is necessary. Keep the scissors sharp by periodically cutting sandpaper with them. Put a hook or magnet on your frame so the scissors will be accessible to you at all times. Scissors with bent handles, like miniature hedge pruners, are perfect for shearing off the tips of loops.

Here are some additional suggestions to make your work easier. You can use a whisk-broom to keep excess yarn and material from your work, but a wet cloth removes small debris more effectively. For light, a gooseneck lamp is useful because it is adjustable and can easily be attached to the frame. Lastly, rub the backing material with paraffin and the hooking will be a lot easier.

Fig. 5-9 A material cutter is a valuable time-saving tool. Short strips take as long to thread as they do to hook. A foot-long strip hooks 3 inches of ½-inch pile and takes five seconds to hook, another five seconds to thread in a Susan Burr hook. Short strips are wonderful for quick color changes and complex patterns, but use long strips from blankets and long pants for hooking in all one color.

Fig. 5-10 Applying latex backing to a rug.

6

Hand Hooking

The photographs at the opening of this chapter (figs. 6-1–6-4) look at first like ancient Peruvian designs woven in an Oriental carpet, but they are hand hooked. The artisan, Eleanor Smoler, used a size 00 steel crochet hook jammed into a handle, strips of woolen materials in their original colors, and heavy rug warp as backing material. The pile is an even ⅜ inch high. None of the work was done on a rug hooking frame, and nothing more than a rough sketch was drawn prior to hooking the rug. The sketch for the stair runner is simply a series of the same crudely shaped figure placed in different positions on red rectangles. The outlines were drawn first on the rug backing, but the elaborate designing was really accomplished in the hooking process. The material that was used was taken from a collection of fabrics Ms. Smoler has amassed over the years. It is the designing that takes time, she says, but to her the hooking was easily and quickly done, even without a frame or regular rug hook.

Many Canadian rugmakers also hook rugs without frames. Either the backing is held in the rug hooker's lap, or the backing is hung off the edge of a table and held in place with a weight.

Fig. 6-1 (*top*)   Stair treads, hand hooked by Eleanor Smoler. They were made without a frame, on rug warp backing, and have a ⅜-inch pile.

Figs. 6-2, 6-3   Details from stair treads.

Fig. 6-4 (*below*)   "Red Rug" (4′ × 6′), hand hooked by Eleanor Smoler. It has a ⅜-inch pile.

Plate 11   Detail of "Rose Rug" (30″ × 61″), hand hooked by Eleanor Smoler. It was made without a frame, from wool strips, and has a ⅜-inch pile.

How to Hand Hook

Hold the yarn or strip of material between thumb and forefinger and stretch it under the backing. With your other hand, push the tip of the rug hook at an angle through the weave of the backing cloth and under the yarn or strip of material. Next, by rolling your hand backward, lift the hook back up through the cloth so a loop is formed (fig. 6-5). Skip two threads of the weave and push the hook through again, pick up another loop, pull up, and disengage the hook. Work from right to left. Try making five ½-inch loops to the inch, then five ¼-inch loops to the inch, and then four 1-inch loops to the inch. You can hook any height of pile you wish. Adjust the spacing

Fig. 6-5   Lift the hook back up through the cloth so a loop is formed.

of the loops and rows according to the height of pile so the rug feels firm and no backing shows from the pile side. Practice pulling all different heights of loops so that you develop a feel for the possible range in rugmaking. Hook a square inch of loops and close your fingers into a tight circle around the loops. This will show you the density of the pile, and you can decide if you want to maintain that height of pile and spacing.

Very high pile should be hooked in rows of alternating heights. One row should be the maximum pile height, and the next row approximately half the maximum.

When your strip of material runs out or when you want to stop hooking a particular strand of yarn, pull up the last loop and cut it so that its end is even with the other loops. The first end of the next strip should be pulled up through this same hole. (See fig. 6-5.) There is no danger of any end pulling out if they are all on the pile side of the rug.

Hook the second and succeeding rows away from you and the loops will not be in your way. Try hooking a spiral, square, or star to discover in which directions you enjoy hooking the most.

Fay Buonocone hooked slipcovers for four chairs with 4-ply knitting yarn and cotton rug yarn. The extremely high pile is so long it literally falls over itself. (See fig. 6-6.) The covers can be taken off the chairs when they have to be cleaned. This is a very effective use of such high pile and the slipcovers look like something made with the rya technique.

The rest of this chapter will be concerned with hems, binding, mitering corners, joining sections of rugs together, and finishing rugs—information that applies to all hooked rugs.

Hems

To keep woven material from unraveling as soon as it's cut, sew a hem along the cut

Fig. 6-6 A chair slipcover, hand hooked by Fay Buonocone.

edge, or affix masking tape to one side, folding over the fraying edge and sealing it to the other side. The hem of a hooked rug should be at least 1½ inches wide. For a large rug the hem can be as wide as 3 inches, especially for square and rectangular rugs. The hem helps to reinforce the edges of the rug. Circular rugs should either be finished with a narrower hem or be bound. All rugs that are tacked to the frame are hemmed after the hooking is finished. To do this, remove the backing from the frame, lay the rug pile-side down, remove any masking tape, and choose one of the following hemming methods:

1. Fold the edge of the material back to the first row of hooking, then fold this back over the hooking and hem in place with double carpet thread.
2. Use a special sealing compound of latex or glue to affix the hem to the rug backing after the rest of the rug has been latexed.
3. For circular or free-form rugs, cut a narrow hem and "pleat" it or ease it around the curves. If it is necessary to cut a wedge, make sure that you sew the edges well on either side to prevent the material from unraveling.

Binding

The alternative to hemming is to bind the edges of a rug with cotton tape, chair webbing, or bias strips (in the case of circular rugs). Burlap-backed rugs should be bound. Binding is more time-consuming than hemming, but you can save some time by machine sewing one edge of the binding to the top side of the rug border. After the rug is hooked, hand sew the other side of the binding to the back side of the rug. If your rug design is considerably smaller than the frame, or if the pattern does not have sufficient excess material on all sides to attach to the frame, sew on a wide strip of sailcloth or binding tape and cut off the excess before sewing the second edge in place.

Edges

Because the edges of a rug receive the hardest wear, the last rows of hooking should be tighter and closer together. You may also want to hook the last row at an angle, pointing toward the edge. When the rug is laid, the edge will turn toward the floor.

Mitered Corners

The hems of square and rectangular rugs present the rugmaker with a double thickness of two hems meeting at each corner. The wider the hem, the more difficult it is to sew. A mitered corner solves the problem in a neat and easy manner.

To make a mitered corner (fig. 6-7), fold both hems back when approaching a corner and make a triangle at the corner with the bottom crease of the triangle crossing the intersection of the hems. Lay the triangle back and cut it off, leaving ½ inch on the corner side of the intersection. Without the triangle, it is easy to fold the two hems so their edges meet. Sew these edges together.

Fig. 6-7   A mitered corner.

Joining and Blending

It is practical for many rugmakers to hook a rug in sections and to join them later to complete the rug. But the more pieces there are, the harder it becomes to fit them together exactly. If a piece is too small, iron its back side to stretch it. Other irregularities may also be ironed out while matching the sections. The best way to join sections is to overlap their edges and hook them together. Make the overlap at least 1½ inches wide, pin the sections evenly, and center this area on the frame. Set the speed hook for a slightly higher pile to compensate for the thickness of the backing. Hook uneven rows across the overlap, and never start or end a row on the joint or at the same place at either end.

This is the same "ragged edge" method that rugmakers employ to blend colors. It is a good idea to combine blending colors and joining sections.

For large sections, lay the hooked pieces with the pile side down and sew the edges together, as you would a seam. You may have to hook some loops in with a hand hook if there are any spaces left near the edge that are visible from the other side.

Finishing

Check the back side of the rug and fix any sparsely hooked areas or ends that have not been pushed to the pile side. Iron any corners that tend to curl up.

Either put the rug on a rubber pad or attach a sailcloth cover to ease the friction that could break the back of the loops when the rug is walked on. You should give some thought to where you place a nonlatexed rug. Little children, pets, or shoes could accidentally pull the loops up. For floor use, the best rug without a latex backing is a close-looped or short-cut pile because there is less danger of the pile coming out. Naturally, a wall hanging has less chance than any rug of having the pile pulled.

Plan to latex your rug on a sunny day or dry night. Stretch the rug out. Latex will seal the loops securely to the backing cloth and make the rug skidproof. A light coat is sufficient; a heavy coat will make the back crack and lessen the rug's pliability. Latex is rubber with a clay filler, which could stain light vinyl and similar surfaces. If your floor might get stained, use a nonrubber pad under the rug.

Plate 12 (*above*) Hand hooked rug (3′ × 6′) by Eleanor Smoler. It was hooked with a crochet hook. Wool strips in their original colors were used on heavy backing, no frame.

Fig. 6-8 A rug (4′ × 5′), hand hooked by Mrs. Lawrence Jonathan of the Six Nations Reserve, Ontario. The rug, with a 2-inch clipped pile, was hooked with wool strips supplied by the Rittermere Crafts Studio. The proprietors taught hooking craftsmanship and design at the Indian reservation for two winters.

7

The Punch Needle

The punch needle is the lightest, smallest, cheapest, and slowest speed hook. Because it is held like a pencil, the rugmaker can easily maneuver it in and out of small places. All the other speed hooks make a click when a loop is made, but the punch needle is absolutely quiet and very relaxing to use.

There are a number of rudimentary punch needles on the market. Yarn is threaded through the eye of the needle shaft and the needle can make one or two pile heights. However, the Columbia-Minerva deluxe punch needle has a more sophisticated construction. There are ten notches in its handle and each notch is for a different height of pile, ranging from 1/4 inch to 3/4 inch. It also has interchangeable points, one for rug yarn, the other for thinner ply yarn. Threading this deluxe needle requires more yarn than any of the other models because the yarn must be put through the screw eye in the handle, down along the shaft and out through the eye of the needle. The yarn must be pulled tightly so that it contracts and fits into the narrow shaft. The needle is twisted into a slot for the desired height of pile and a serrated sliding lock is pulled down to hold the tip in place. Quick changes of color or spots are better hooked with the shuttle hook or with a simpler model punch needle. The #10 setting is for the lowest pile, #5 is for a ½-inch pile, and #1 is for the highest, a ¾-inch pile.

How to Punch Hook

Face the open end of the punch needle with the threaded yarn in the direction you are going to hook. This open point must always lead in order for the yarn to make loops. Hold the needle vertically between your thumb and forefinger. With the hand not holding the punch needle, pull some yarn from the tip of the needle so that it extends an inch (fig. 7-1). Push the needle down through the weave of the backing cloth so that the base of the handle or wire gauge touches the cloth (fig. 7-2). Reach under the frame and hold onto the extended piece of yarn. Pull the punch needle up, go forward two threads, push the needle down again and let go of the end of yarn. Pull the hook up again and you have made a loop. Barely lifting the punch needle up from the backing cloth, glide it gently at a slight slant into the next space. Your other hand has only to hold the first end of yarn down in order to have some "anchor" before the hooking begins. As with all hooking techniques, all ends must be poked through to the pile side.

The time it takes to hook a rug depends entirely on the height and density of the pile, color changes, the complexity of the pattern, and your manual dexterity. For an experienced rugmaker, it can take an hour to complete a square foot of rug punch hooking. The be-

ginner should concentrate on getting the rhythm of the punch needle technique rather than speed. The operation of the punch needle eventually will become automatic and natural, and speed will increase with experience.

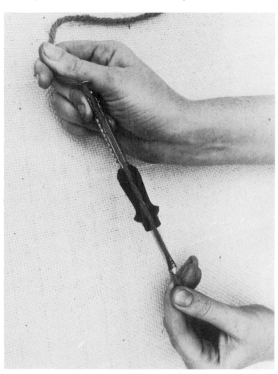

Fig. 7-1 Pull yarn from the tip of the needle so that it extends an inch.

Fig. 7-2 Hold the punch needle like a pencil and push it down through the burlap backing all the way to the shaft handle. Then pull the hook out and a loop is formed on underside of rug.

Sometimes the tip of the needle will be difficult to push through a couple of threads and instead of breaking the weave, the tip will dislodge from the notch and slide up, thus producing a very short loop. If this happens, be sure to tighten the material so that the weave is stretched out. Also, make sure that the point is between the threads of the cloth before pushing it down. If the point of the punch needle ever gets dull, sharpen it with an emery board.

"The Knight and Castles" (figs. 7-3 and 7-4) and "The Pond" (fig. 7-6) are examples of George Wells' artistry and craftsmanship. Wells has made over five thousand rugs in 17 years, most of them employing the punch needle technique. Most of his rugs are made at the lowest setting—¼-inch pile—on the deluxe needle. The watercolor sketch is of "The Pond" (fig. 7-5), which is in the hall area of the Stephen Smith residence in Hyannisport, Massachusetts. The work was commissioned by McMillen, Inc. A detail from the rug demonstrates the accuracy of his technique. The colors in both examples are dyed with his special Craftsman's dyes. The yarn he uses is acidified to take the dye in hot tap water.

Fig. 7-4 Detail from "The Knight and Castles" rug.

Fig. 7-3 "The Knight and Castles" rug (13′ × 14′), hand hooked by George Wells. It was hooked with hand-dyed wool yarn. The background is in shades of gold.

Plate 13 "Pastorale," a hooked rug by George Wells.

The low ¼-inch pile that is necessary for details in representational rugs is also essential for the clarification of abstract designs, as is illustrated in the work of Bruce Duderstadt (figs. 7-7–7-10). The pile, hooked with an ordinary punch needle, is hooked in order to emphasize the shapes in the design: the circles are hooked in circles, the lines in straight rows, and so forth.

A higher pile gives a different dimension to the design. The square wall hanging by Bruce Duderstadt, which is owned by the San Antonio Art League (fig. 7-10) is a good example of the use of pile. The size of the work contributes immensely to one's awareness of the pile. The size of Duderstadt's hanging (fig. 7-8) for the Bank of San Antonio makes it almost impossible to distinguish the low pile.

To Bruce Duderstadt's way of thinking, the beauty of a rug's back is equal to its front. He believes that if a rug is to be hung, as all of his are, the back should not be latexed. Latexing discolors and obscures the pattern of loops. Furthermore, he has a way of hemming which does not cover any part of the rug. His method makes it easy to repair any dislodged loops along the edges, and the hem doesn't look obtrusive. This is how he describes his method: "I cut the cotton backing about 2½ inches from the last row of loops, roll or fold the backing under twice, then bind it with a buttonhole stitch in white or colored yarn. At the top I wrap a metal rod with the backing and then bind it."

The texture of hooked yarn is more overt when the color is not emphasized and a definite pattern of contrasting pile heights is maintained. There are three "Winterdrawings" hooked by Hildegarde Klene from pictures by the sculptor José Bermudez. All of them are the same size and each design is developed by the varying textures of the hooked yarn. The first "Winterdrawing" (fig. 7-11) has two rows of black lines in the center. "Winterdrawing 11" (fig. 7-12–7-14) is all white and the background is hooked with the #7 (⁷⁄₁₆ inch)

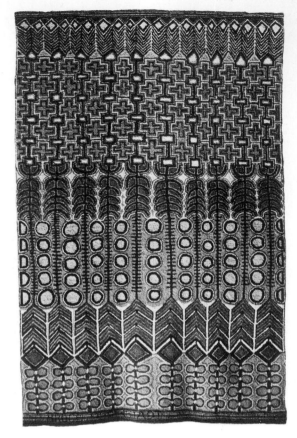

Fig. 7-5 (*top left*) A watercolor sketch of "The Pond," a rug (9'4" × 12'9") made for the Stephen Smith residence in Hyannisport, Mass., and hooked and designed by George Wells for McMillen, Inc.

Fig. 7-6 (*left*) Detail of "The Pond."

Fig. 7-7 "Horizontal Patterns," 1970 (5' × 7½'), a punch needle wall hanging by Bruce Duderstadt. It has ¼-inch wool yarn pile.

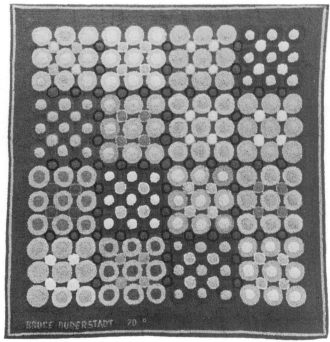

Fig. 7-8 (*top left*) Wall hanging for the Bank of San Antonio, 1972 (8½′ × 15′) by Bruce Duderstadt. It has a $\frac{3}{16}$-inch pile with rows $\frac{3}{16}$ inch apart.

Fig. 7-9 Punch needle wall hanging, 1971 (5½′ square) by Bruce Duderstadt. It has a 1-inch pile with rows ½ inch apart.

Fig. 7-10 (*right*) Punch needle wall hanging (4½′ × 4½′) by Bruce Duderstadt. It has a ¼-inch pile and ¼ pound wool yarn was used per square foot. This work is owned by the San Antonio Art League.

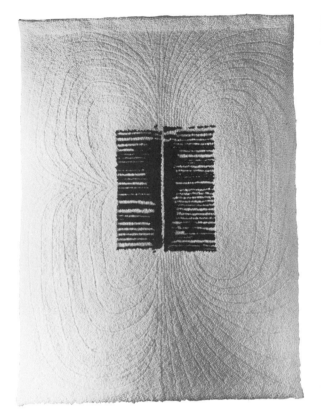

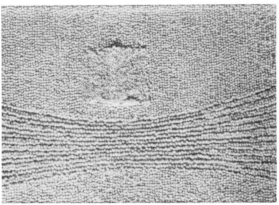

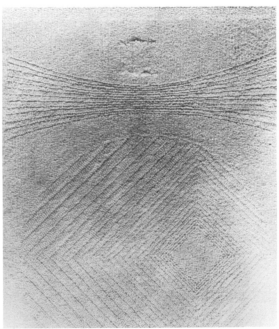

Fig. 7-11 (*top left*) "Winterdrawing" (42″ × 60″), punch needle hanging by Hildegarde Klene. Made from a design drawn by the sculptor José Bermudez, the hanging has low and high uncut pile.

Fig. 7-12 (*left*) "Winterdrawing II" (42″ × 60″), a punch needle hanging by Hildegarde Klene.

Figs. 7-13, 7-14 Details of "Winterdrawing II."

setting of the deluxe punch needle. The third "Winterdrawing," not shown here, has white half-circles cut in the middle with a red and black stripe. The yarn in "Crater" (fig. 7-15), "Desert" (color plate 14), and "Rushes in a Watery Place" (fig. 7-17) was dyed by Ms. Klene with Craftsman's dyes bought at George Wells' store, The Ruggery.

Yarn is almost always used in the punch needle because material often snags in the shaft. Gloria Crouse, however, has had much success punch hooking ¼-inch strips of velvet, wool, and especially cotton (figs. 7-19–7-21, color plate 15). She makes a small crayon or chalk sketch of her idea and then, from her collection of remnants, selects some material, which she cuts into strips with her machine cutter. For closely shaped pile she prefers to use 4-ply knitting worsted hooked very tightly, which she then shapes with scissors to the desired sculpted form. Notice how the cloth looks both cut and uncut in the detail of her pillow—how different it is from yarn!

The work of Silvia Heyden (fig. 7-18) is a departure from the usual methods of the punch needle rugmaker. Ms. Heyden first did many drawings, watercolors, and collages that emphasized texture and design. After this preparation, she hooked the hanging in an even high pile on a frame made from a table without its top. When she finished, she turned her work over and hooked additional pile in the spaces between the original rows. Hence, there is pile on the back. This reverse method of rug hooking requires an enormous amount of additional time, but the result is singularly beautiful.

Plate 14   "Desert" by Hildegarde Klene. Made with the punch needle technique.

Fig. 7-15 (*above*) "Crater," a punch needle hanging by Hildegarde Klene.

Fig. 7-16 "Leaf" (8" × 11"), a punch needle hanging by Hildegarde Klene.

54

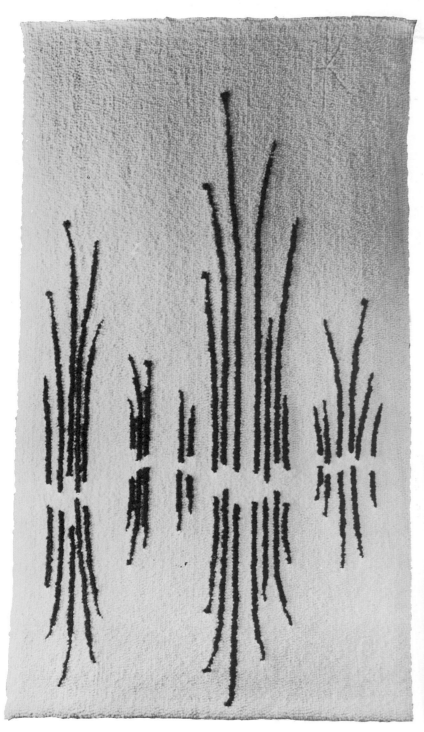

Fig. 7-17 (*left*) "Rushes in a Watery Place" (42" × 72"), a white, brown, and black punch needle wall hanging by Hildegarde Klene.

Fig. 7-18 "Los Americanos" (5' × 7') by Silvia Heyden. It was made with punch needle and reverse hooking technique.

Fig. 7-19 (*above*) "Patchwork Pillow," punch hooked with ¼-inch cloth strips by Gloria Crouse.

Fig. 7-20 Detail of "Patchwork Pillow."

56

Plate 15 "Autumn," punch hooked with sheared and shaped knitting yarn by Gloria Crouse.

Fig. 7-21 "On the Rocks" (27″ square), made with ¼-inch cotton strips punch needle hooked in a 1-inch pile by Gloria Crouse.

8

The Shuttle Hook

The flat wooden handle of the shuttle hook is split into two sections which you push and pull back and forth to hook the yarn or material through the backing material. The needle is attached to one section of the handle, the looper to the other. When the needle has been pushed down and the height of the loop is established, it is pulled up while the other side with the looper is pushed down, holding the loop in place. When the needle is pulled completely back, it automatically moves on to the next space. The shuttle hook is worked either vertically or horizontally and every time a loop is made a click is heard. (See figs. 8-1–8-4.)

There are three reasons for the popularity of the shuttle hook, which was invented in the 1880s: first, it is easy to thread; second, short strips of material can be used as easily as

58

long; and third, the shuttle hook can be moved along very quickly to speed the progress of rugmaking.

The shuttle hook originated in Scotland and according to the Mills-Mossellers, rugmakers in North Carolina, the technique is still called "thrumcrofting" in the South.

Of the two shuttle hooks available today, the Susan Burr and the Tru-Gyde, I prefer the Tru-Gyde. The Susan Burr, which is shaped somewhat like a guitar, makes one even-height pile of ½ inch.

The Tru-Gyde is larger and more rectangular than the Susan Burr. In addition to a large point with three settings for strips of material (⅜ inch, ⁹⁄₁₆ inch, and ¾ inch), there is a small point just for rug yarn, and it has four settings (¼ inch, ⁷⁄₁₆ inch, ⅝ inch, and ⅞ inch). For each setting, the Tru-Gyde needs to be dismantled and the looper readjusted with the needle, but it is worth the effort.

When you first get the shuttle hook, move the sections back and forth to get the feel of it. During humid weather the wood might stick, but a rubbing with paraffin makes it work easily. Hold the sides lightly and position your fingers so that the shuttle hook will move at an oblique angle (approximately forty-five degrees) to the stretched backing material. If a shuttle hook is worked on too great a slant, the loops will be uneven and farther apart than they should be. Using either a strip of material or a piece of rug yarn, thread the shuttle hook through the screw eye on the wooden section and out through the eye of the needle about 2 inches (fig. 8-2). Push the needle section down through backing material until wooden handle touches the cloth (fig. 8-3). As you pull it back up, push the looper down, and it will go into same hole as the needle (fig. 8-4). This holds the loop while the needle is withdrawn. When the needle is pulled all the way up, it automatically moves ahead. Always face the shuttle hook in the direction you want to hook. Cut the last loop right above

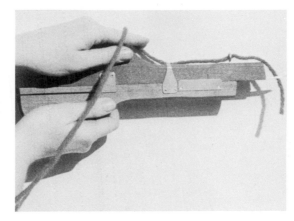

Fig. 8-1 Holding the shuttle hook.

the backing material and push the end back through the hole. Start the next piece in this same hole.

When you have hooked a few rows, check to see that the pile is spaced correctly and that it is all the same height. There should be four or five loops to the inch. If there are fewer, you are probably slanting the shuttle hook too much, or perhaps the backing isn't tight enough.

The looper is aligned precisely with the needle point. If either should become bent, be sure to adjust them, or return them to the manufacturer, who will re-align them at a reasonable price. They will not function properly if they are not aligned correctly. Sharpen the needle with an emery board.

One rugmaker, a thirteen-year-old, advises hooking every other row and working the rows in between afterward. This way you are able to finish straighter rows in a shorter time. The shuttle hook is a rather large rugmaking tool, and the movement of the handles makes it difficult to see the exact placement of every loop.

In order to change direction with the shuttle hook, pivot it when the looper is down through the backing and the needle is pulled up.

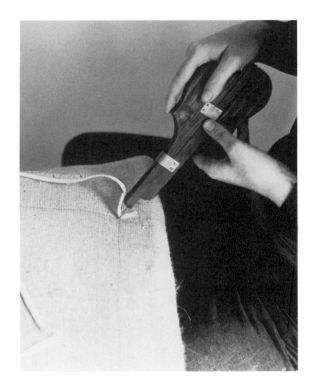

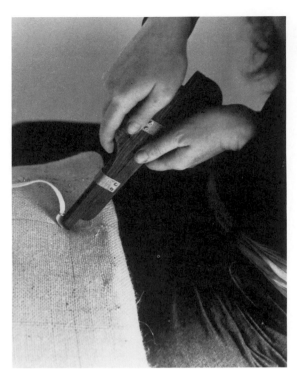

Fig. 8-2 (*top left*) After threading the hook through the screw eye and eye of the needle, extend the yarn or material about 2 inches through the eye of the needle.

Fig. 8-3 (*top right*) Push the needle side of the shuttle hook down through the backing.

Fig. 8-4 Now push the looper side of the shuttle hook down and the needle side will come up, automatically moving to the next space and ready for the next loop.

Fig. 8-5 (*right*) "Le Fiacre," shuttle hooked by Ronald Mosseller (Romne).

Fig. 8-6 Buffalo herd rug commissioned by the Kleheig's King Ranch, Texas, and "thrumcrofted" by the Mills-Mossellers.

61

Fig. 8-7 Detail of clouds, shuttle hooked by Romne, from "Supersonic Transport."

Table 5 gives the dimensions of an area that can be hooked with strips of material. Note that the settings apply to the large needle point at the settings available on the Tru-Gyde. The figures cannot be absolutely accurate but will be of help to any rugmaker using material. The information in the table has been adapted from information given in the Tru-Gyde catalog.

Table 5

Material (1 sq. yd.)	Setting #1 3/8-in. pile
cotton, flannel sheets, light blankets: 5/8-in. wide strips	8 in. by 8 in.
silk, rayon, broadcloth, gingham, percale: 3/4-in. wide strips	7 in. by 7 in.
extra heavy wool coats, blankets: 1/4-in. wide strips	12 in. by 14 in.
suits, coats, dresses: 1/2-in. wide strips	9 in. by 9 in.

Higher pile requires more material:

$\frac{9}{16}$-inch pile (#2 setting) requires 50 percent more material than you would use for 3/8-inch pile (#1 setting).

3/4-inch pile (#3 setting) requires 85 percent more material than necessary for #1 setting.

When Lillian Mills-Mosseller, many years ago, saw the hooked rugs made by Appalachian craftsmen, she told a local newspaper reporter: "They were all the same design, which I soon got sick of. So I volunteered to make some new designs for one mountain woman who said she'd be glad to get them. So I gave her some. Then came her next batch of rugs. They were the same old designs. I asked her why she hadn't used the new designs. She said she couldn't dye the yarn the right colors for the pictures. I helped her dye the yarn the right colors, and that's how I got started in the rug business."

Since that time, she and her son, Ronald Mosseller, have shown their "paintings in wool" paired with the oil originals at a New York gallery and have created numerous period-piece carpets for governors' mansions and other large residences, as well as carpets commissioned for several presidential rooms at the Smithsonian Institution.

The pile on their carpets is always very dense—a square foot is shuttle hooked with a full pound of yarn. The pile is usually sheared with modified sheep shears to an even inch pile. Some of the wool is imported from Australia and Scotland, then spun to their specifications in this country. They dye all the yarn themselves with Du Pont dyes. Sometimes there are hundreds of colors in a single work.

Fig. 8-8 (*left*) "Texas Star and Trees," a shuttle hooked rug by Romne.

Fig. 8-9 (*above*) Stuffed lion, designed by Romne for *Woman's Day* magazine, 1971. Patterns available from Crafts Editor.

Fig. 8-10 Shuttle hooked Regency dining room rug, designed and executed by Romne for the Williamsburg Inn, Williamsburg, Virginia.

Fig. 8-11 "Hamiltonian" rug by Romne, after the painting by George Stubbs, 1799.

In the 1960s a new form of rugmaking called "rag tapestries" was initiated by Ann Wiseman. Her first workshop was sponsored by the Stuart Country Day School of Princeton, New Jersey, in 1965. Sixty girls, ten to fifteen years old, signed up for the workshop. Their first work, a rag tapestry 4 feet by 12 feet, was called "The Beginning of the Beginning." (See fig. 8-12, color plates 6, 17, 18.)

Once the girls decided on a theme and chose a title, they drew and cut out flowers, animals, birds, and foliage and assembled them on large sheets of brown wrapping paper. The figures' contours were traced and the lines were redrawn with charcoal. To prevent the charcoal from smudging when the design was transferred to the backing material, several girls held the paper on all sides, lowered it to within an inch of the backing, and dropped it into place. The charcoal was pressed into the backing and all lines were copied with indelible markers. The backing was then hemmed and laced to the vertical frame.

Seventy-five pounds of woolen clothes and material in all colors and patterns were donated to the project. The selected material was cut up into ¼-inch strips. Twelve members of the workshop worked on the tapestry with Susan Burr hooks. Others prepared and cut strips of cloth or made lap samplers with regular hand hooks.

"The Beginning of the Beginning" received a great deal of attention. The Metropolitan Museum of Art in New York City invited the children to bring it in, and for six months it was on exhibit in the children's library of the museum.

The success of the first rag tapestry led to the making of another tapestry at the school. "The Epic of Gilgamesh," 4 feet by 12 feet, was completed in 1967. That year Ann Wiseman also conducted a workshop for children eight to twelve years old at the Metropolitan Museum of Art. The tapestry that the children made is 4 feet by 10 feet and depicts New York City (fig. 8-13). It now hangs at the children's entrance to the museum. A short

Plate 16 "North Carolina Garden," shuttle hooked by Romne.

16mm color documentary about this project, called *New York—A Rag Tapestry by 25 Children,* is available from the International Film Foundation, 475 Fifth Avenue, New York City.

While acting as program director of the Children's Museum in Boston, Ann Wiseman set up a tapestry in the visitors' center that was hooked (and unhooked!) by two thousand visitors to the museum over a period of six months. The following year school children in Roxbury, under Ms. Wiseman's direction, completed a tapestry project sponsored by the Massachusetts Council on the Arts and Humanities and the Boston Museum of Fine Arts. This tapestry, "City of the Future," illustrates the children's fantasies about the future. It was hung in the Boston Museum of Fine Arts and was accompanied by a slide-talk in which the children explained what they were doing.

Ms. Wiseman was trained as a painter, an experience which, along with her tapestry making, gave birth to the concept of the rag tapestry. There has since been ample evidence of the success of her idea. Both the film and her books have encouraged people here and abroad to hook rag tapestries.

A rag tapestry is the logical extension of the mural. It can be of any size and can involve any number of participants of any age. The materials used are secondhand clothes and remnants, which are good for both budgetary and ecological reasons. Furthermore, shuttle hooking a rag tapestry is an engrossing cooperative effort. A tapestry that is hung in a classroom or in a public place will absorb a great deal of noise. Beyond the practical benefits, a rag tapestry is a unique and imaginative medium that deserves to be explored further.

Fig. 8-12 "The Beginning of the Beginning," 1966 (4′ × 12′), rag tapestry shuttle hooked by school children of the Stuart Country Day School in Princeton, N.J. The children used Susan Burr hooks, strips of cloth ¼-inch wide, and worked under the supervision of Ann Wiseman.

Plates 17, 18   Details of "The Beginning of the Beginning."

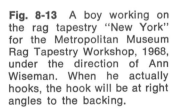

Fig. 8-13 A boy working on the rag tapestry "New York" for the Metropolitan Museum Rag Tapestry Workshop, 1968, under the direction of Ann Wiseman. When he actually hooks, the hook will be at right angles to the backing.

Fig. 8-14 "Leopard Family," hooked with a Susan Burr hook by Ann Wiseman.

Fig. 8-15 Shuttle hooked tapestry (10′ × 25′) in progress for Wellesely Hospital in Toronto, 1966, by Grace Svarre.

Plate 19 Shuttle hooked tapestry (5′ × 20′6″) by Grace Svarre. It was made for the Laidlow Library at the University of Toronto and was completed in three months. The pile is ¼ to 2 inches high with very close spacing.

Plate 20 Shuttle hooked hanging (3′ × 7′), 1965, by Grace Svarre.

70

Plate 21 Shuttle hooked hanging (2' × 4'6"), 1965, by Grace Svarre.

Fig. 8-16   Shuttle hooked hanging by Grace Svarre.

Plate 22   Shuttle hooked hanging (4′ × 6′), 1965, by Grace Svarre.

9

Other Speed Hooks

The speed tufting tool is a new rug hook that has recently come into vogue. Originally it cost five times as much as the deluxe punch needle and twice as much as the Tru-Gyde. However, a five-dollar model is now available. As with other speed hooks, the pile is hooked through the backing material, which is stretched on a horizontal or vertical frame. What is different about the tufting tool is that the looper is attached to a lever which is moved back and forth to make the pile and automatically space the loops. With a little practice, a square foot can be hooked in a half hour to three-quarters of an hour. Three heights are marked on the looper for convenience, but pile can be hooked to any height from $1/8$ inch to $1\frac{1}{2}$ inches.

To thread the speed tufting tool, bend a piece of wire in half and insert the bent end through the needle shaft toward the handle of the tool. Put the end of yarn through the bend and pull the wire back through the shaft (fig. 9-2). Remove the wire and keep it stuck into the rug backing so that it will be easy to find when the next piece of yarn is needed.

Hold the tufting tool at right angles to the backing; have one hand on the handle, the other holding the lever back (fig. 9-1). Pull the first end of yarn out an inch and penetrate the cloth with the needle. Pushing the lever down raises the needle and automatically spaces the next loop. The looper enters the same hole as the needle and forms a loop in the yarn. Pull the lever back, the needle penetrates the cloth again and another loop is ready to be made.

The tool must be kept lubricated so that it will move easily. If the looper gets bent, it will not be able to follow the needle into the hole and will stick in the cloth. If this happens, push up on the looper so that it is again close to the underside of the needle shaft as it was originally. The tip of the looper must be bent up in order to function properly.

Speed is dependent on how fast the lever can be moved up and down. Some people find it easier to move one lever than to alternate the two handles of the shuttle hook.

The construction of the speed tufting tool is like that of the "Bluenose" rug hooker (fig. 9-3), which is still available in small quantities from a few suppliers. The "Bluenose" is an excellent rug hook. If you own one but don't know how to use it properly, contact George Wells at The Ruggery or Jules Kliot at Some Place (see pages 133–134 for the addresses of suppliers).

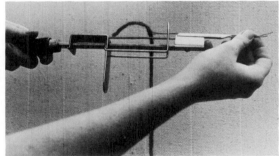

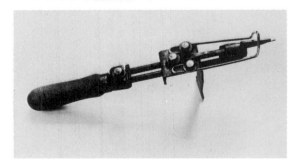

Fig. 9-1 (*top*)   A speed tufting tool is held this way. The lever is moved up and down.

Fig. 9-2 (*center*)   Threading Rugcrafter's speed tufting tool.

Fig. 9-3   The Bluenose rug hook.

The Norcraft Speed Rug Needle, also called the "eggbeater" because of its appearance, makes loops on the opposite side of the stretched backing from the side you are working on. All of the loops are very low, and only from three to five ounces of thin 4-ply yarn per square foot is needed. This is approximately half the amount that is used in most pile rugs. The company that sells this needle, Norden Needle Crafts Company, claims that it is possible to hook up to five hundred loops a minute, or an average of a square foot in less than ten minutes. I tried hooking with the "eggbeater" and had a hard time making the loops stay in the weave of the cloth at any speed. The design of the "eggbeater" is innovative and in time could become a tool of great ad-vantage to rug hookers. But, as of now, due to the thin yarn and pile height required, I don't recommend it for hooking high-pile rugs as described in this book.

The D'Kor Electric Needle operates with downward pressure. The company that makes this device claims that their needle can make up to five hundred loops per minute, or six square feet in an hour, for a plain rug in one color. The height of the pile can be adjusted from $\frac{1}{8}$ inch to 1 inch. The D'Kor Electric Needle is available in a kit that includes a frame, yarn, and a pattern, and costs about forty dollars. It is for the professional who is hooking large rugs and has arms strong enough to be able to guide the machine correctly.

Fig. 9-4 "Gray and White Arrows" (34″ × 53″) by Marla Mallett. *Collection of Southern Belle, Atlanta, Ga.*

Fig. 9-5 (*above*) "Blue and Ochre," 1968 (30″ × 66″), a tufted rug by Marla Mallett.

Fig. 9-6 "Red-Brown Medallion" (5′ × 5′), a tufted rug by Marla Mallett.

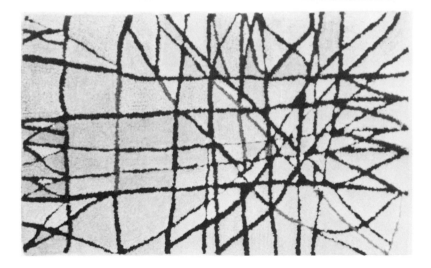

Fig. 9-7 (*top*) "Green" (41″ × 66″), a speed hooked rug by Marla Mallett.

Fig. 9-8 (*center*) "Red and Blue Stripes" (4′ × 6′), a rug by Marla Mallett.

Fig. 9-9 "Brown Furrows" (45″ × 70″), a rug hooked with yarn and cut wool strips by Marla Mallett. (See fig. 4-4, page 29 for a detail of this rug.)

78

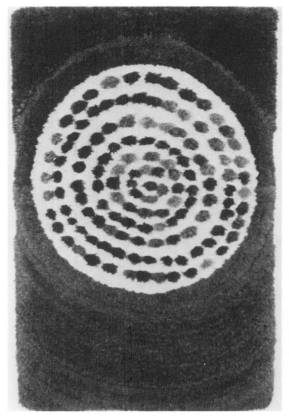

Plate 23 (*top*) "Red Spot" (41″ × 70″), a rug tufted by Marla Mallett. A punch needle was used.

Fig. 9-10 (*right*) "Circuit" (42″ × 64″), a rug by Marla Mallett.

Fig. 9-11 Detail of "Circuit."

10

The Latch Hook Technique

The latch hook originated in the British Isles, as did the hand hook and the shuttle hook. But unlike the other two, the latch hook has yet to become very popular with the majority of American rugmakers. Latch hooking does, however, prevail among the rugmakers of Great Britain, Australia, and Canada to such an extent that suppliers in those nations sell latch hooks almost to the exclusion of other rugmaking tools.

A latch hooked rug is made by cutting and folding a piece of yarn around the latch hook and knotting the yarn to mesh backing material so that the ends of the yarn stick up to form the pile.

There are special advantages to the latch hook technique. The mesh backing is composed of evenly spaced holes, and a latch hook knot is tied through each hole. Two sizes of mesh are available: eleven or sixteen holes per square inch. The cut pile looks different from the sheared pile of rugs made with other hooking methods; the density of the pile is not as great, so the rug has a tufted shag appearance.

Because the pile is cut prior to knotting, it can be cut evenly or in a variety of heights, and because individual pieces of yarn are knotted, a different color can be knotted in each hole of the mesh. An example in its fullest application would be a rug resembling an impressionist painting where the principle of pointillism applies. Latch hook knots in a variety of colors can form spots of color to convey space and form. The use of muted related shades could simulate a Monet; larger brighter spots of color for more perspective and movement could simulate a Seurat.

If you use the latch hook technique, you can make a rug in sections on your lap. There is nothing to set up; your work is portable. You can cut enough yarn to cover an area likely to be worked in a certain amount of time and then roll up the canvas when you are finished. The evenly spaced mesh simplifies completing the rug.

The rug is hemmed as it is made. The hem is folded back onto the rug canvas, and this double layer is knotted through. The hems are strong and the double layer of canvas gives additional protection to the edges of the rug.

A latch hooked rug is extremely durable because the backing not only holds its shape while you are working on it, but does so for many years afterward. Dirt sifts down through the holes in the backing onto the floor. This minimizes the necessity of cleaning the rug. No latex is ever needed. I know someone who recently changed a color in a part of her rug after ten years. The knots were easily removed and replaced. Stains, too, can be totally eliminated in this way.

Making latch hooked rugs is a very enjoyable, relaxing, and satisfying form of rugmaking. And although it takes a long time to make

a latch hooked rug, its portability, its pre-cut pile, its knotted hem, and no latexing must be taken into account.

Rug Canvas, or Scrim

Rug canvas, or scrim, is a plastic-coated cotton mesh backing that has either 3⅓ or 4 holes per inch (fig. 10-3). I prefer the former size, which is sold by the yard in widths from 14 to 60 inches. The usual size backings are 32 and 42 inches wide. I recommend the 28-inch-wide scrim because it is usually easier to finish several small sections than one very large one.

The smaller size mesh of four holes per inch is usually only available in 42-inch widths. The threads of the mesh are slightly apart and the holes are harder to distinguish. But for a rug with a closer pile of sixteen knots per square inch, this is the rug canvas to use.

Rug canvas often comes with stenciled lines

Fig. 10-1 Rug designed by Ivan Chermayeff using the latch hook technique.

three inches apart for transferring patterns and for making it easier to determine the amount of yarn needed in each area.

Yarn

A thicker rug yarn is preferred for latch hooking. Wool that is 5- or 6-ply or a combination of several strands of synthetic yarn is best. See Chapter 5 for more specific information about wool yarn and synthetics.

Latch hooking is the one technique for which thick handspun yarn is especially well suited. If you have some, or can get it, I highly recommend experimenting with it. It produces a rough, varied texture that looks good in contrast to the regular, smooth commercial yarn. When you cut the handspun yarn, remember the two ends have to be pulled together through a small square hole. Use the larger size mesh and juggle the wool so that two irregular thicknesses are matched and are easy to pull through the mesh and knot.

Before you order yarn, consider the method you will use to cut it. A loose skein has from forty to sixty strands lying side by side; these can be cut with scissors in a short time, although every strand will not be exactly even in length. Cut one side of the skein near one of the two ties that hold the skein together. Spread the yarn out on a table top, measure the length of twice the pile height plus ½ inch for the knot, and cut it. This method is very easy and since you cut the yarn as you go along, you avoid having unused pieces lying around. Or for a slightly more uneven pile, hold the skein loosely in your hand and cut the yarn all together in one bunch (fig. 10-4).

Most synthetic yarns and some brands of wool rug yarn are sold in pull skeins. Loose skein rug yarn has to be wound in a ball before it can be cut with one of the commercial yarn cutters listed below.

The Emile Bernat Company has a commercial yarn cutter that cuts yarn to one length,

Fig. 10-2 (*above*) Latch hooked rug designed by Jimmy Ernst.

Fig. 10-3 A latch hook with two types of rug canvas, 3⅓ holes to the inch and 4 holes to the inch.

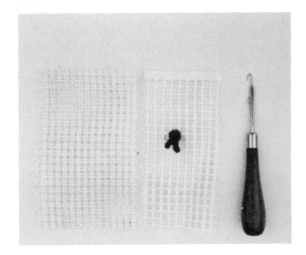

which will give you a uniform 1¼-inch pile.

Another cutter, which is suitable for cutting large amounts of yarn to any desired length of pile, is available from Some Place, a store in Berkeley, California. This cutter is run off an electric drill and would be the obvious choice of someone contemplating a mammoth rug or who was seriously involved commercially in the latch hook technique. I have never had an opportunity to use this cutter.

Harley Jensen, a California architect who has made latch hooked rugs since 1967, devised a method for cutting yarn from a pull skein. He takes a 14-inch piece of wood with a circumference the same as the length of pile he wants—for example, 5 inches for a pile of 2¼ inches—and attaches this to a motor so it revolves. The yarn is fed onto the piece of wood for several layers, then cut with a razor blade. The pieces are tied together with a rubber band until they are used. He says that he can cut all the yarn he needs for a rug in a short time.

To determine what length of yarn to cut for the pile, measure twice the height of the pile and add ½ inch for the knot. For a 1-inch pile, cut the yarn 2½ inches long.

You can also make a cardboard gauge with a width equal to double the pile height plus ½ inch for the knot. Fold the cardboard in half, wrap the yarn around in one layer for an even pile, several for a more uneven pile, and cut through the loops along the open side of the gauge.

Precut yarn is sold for latch hooked rugs. Five packages cover one square foot with a 1¼-inch pile.

How to Latch Hook

This method of latch hooking is to be used by someone working alone: Lay the rug canvas down flat in front of you. Fold a piece of yarn in half around the bottom of the steel shaft with the open latch facing the yarn ends. In-

Fig. 10-4 Cutting yarn for latch hooking.

sert the hook sideways down through one hole and up through the next hole. Push the hook through halfway (fig. 10-5). Twist the handle so that the latch hook is facing up and the latch opens. If the latch doesn't open (it will with practice although you might have some trouble at first), open it with your finger. With your other hand place both yarn ends over the latch opening facing the same direction and hold the ends taut (fig. 10–6).

Pull back on the handle, making sure that all the yarn is secure under the closed latch. If you don't get all the yarn under the latch, it will not be possible to pull the ends through.

Keep your wrist down and lift your hand, flipping the hook up (fig. 10-7). The yarn ends come back through the first hole and the knot is completed. If you keep your wrist up and pull the handle, the knot forms too soon and it will be almost impossible to pull, as the ends are tied in with the knot. Also the mesh will pull out of shape.

It is best to be consistent and work in one direction, from side to side or up and down. The easiest method is to knot in rows (right-left, left-right), each one farther away from you, so the ends won't get in your way. If you switch the side of the hole you knot on, the threads of the mesh pull, which distorts the spacing and makes the knotting harder to do.

Even if the backing was made of wire, changing the direction of the knotting would reflect in the lay of the pile. Individually the pile is vertical, but as a composition of thousands of yarn ends it remains vertical only because the ends are packed together. If you skip a space, the knotted pile will bend over and detract from the uniform density of the rug.

A reverse method of latch hooking applies when two people are working on the same rug. While one person can latch hook in the first way, another person may work on the same rug from the opposite end using a reverse knotting method so that the lay of the pile is consistent. The reverse method is as follows: Push the hook down through one square of the canvas and up into the next square beyond. Twist so that the latch falls open (fig. 10-8). Loop the folded piece of yarn into the open hook and hold it firmly from the top with the ends even (fig. 10-9). Pull back on the handle so that the latch closes and the loop of yarn comes up through the first square of the mesh canvas (fig. 10-10).

Push the latch hook out of the loop and push the ends through to one side through the open latch. Pull back on the latch hook so that the yarn ends go under the loop and lift the pile up.

Fig. 10-5   Fold yarn double around shank of hook.

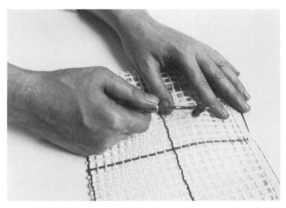

Fig. 10-6   With the lever open, cross both yarn ends over.

Fig. 10-7   A short piece of yarn is easier to knot—longer ends tend to get into the knot. When you pull the knot through, keep wrist down and flip hook up.

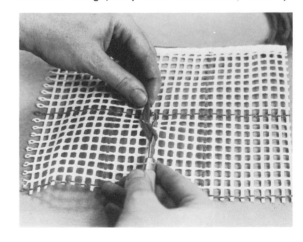

Edges

The edges of a rug wear out more quickly than the body because they are stepped on harder and more frequently. The neat strong edges of a latch hooked rug are made to be very durable. They are simply the raw edges of the rug canvas folded back onto the rest of the backing. Some rugmakers fold the edges up so that the back of the rug looks uniform; others fold the edges under to withstand extra wear next to the floor. You may first want to machine sew the raw edges along the third mesh row to facilitate the knotting.

The size of the folded-back edge should be commensurate with the size of the rug, but at least 1½ inches wide. When you fold the edge back, follow a thread in the mesh so the holes will match evenly. Skip the single thread nearest the raw edge because it will unravel if you try to knot it. At the corners where two edges have to be folded one on top of the other, the thickness makes knotting difficult, but don't cut part of the corner out because a cut alters the stability of the whole rug canvas and the mesh will start to unravel. To deal with this unwieldy thickness, fold one hem up and the other under. It is then easier to knot through.

Elliptical and freeform rugs, like the works of Traute Ishida, are hemmed or bound. The pattern is cut an inch or so out from the last knotted row and the edge is folded back and hemmed, or a binding is sewn on and secured to the rug back.

Square and rectangular rugs are pleasant to make because they can be made in small sections, which can easily be joined together. To join sections, stop knotting each section at least 1½ inches from the edge, overlap the adjoining section's unknotted rows and knot through them both. Make sure that the holes are aligned. There will be a slight ridge because of this double layer of canvas. The ridge is considerably more noticeable with solid colors than with mottled colors and less notice-

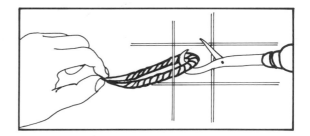

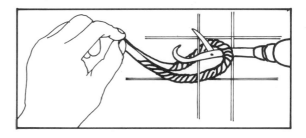

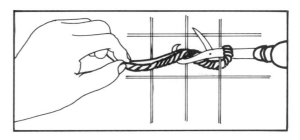

Figs. 10-8–10-10 The reverse method of latch hooking.

able if it coincides with the lines of a design. The ridge can be modified by cutting the pile a fraction of an inch shorter in the overlap.

Or the selvages of sections can be sewn together. If the rug is small enough, it can be done on a sewing machine. Hold the bound edges together and sew them as close to the mesh as you can. Fold them back like a seam; the weight of the rug will keep them down flat.

Definition of Line and Space

To make a line stand out as clearly as possible, cut the pile for this line slightly longer, or that of the adjacent rows a little shorter. If the line is of a shorter pile, it will seem narrower and more contained. If it is higher pile, it will look thicker because the tufts will spread out more.

For defining spaces such as circles and triangles, make the shape by increasing and decreasing the number of knots per row. For example, a circle would begin with a row of only a few knots. Each successive row would have more knots until you reach the middle of the circle. The knots should decrease in the same order. (See figs. 10-11, 10-12.)

Two variations of the latch hook technique make it comparable in work time to other rug-making methods.

Method 1—The checkerboard rug (figs. 10-13, 10-14). Stagger the knots so that every other hole is knotted, and use at least a 1½-inch pile. The rug will not be as firm or as durable as a fully knotted rug, but it will be lighter, take half the time, half the work, half the yarn, and the dirt shakes out well. This is most suitable for wall hangings and for floor areas without a lot of traffic. Use mesh with three-and-one-third holes per inch.

Method 2—Speed hook some areas of the rug by stretching the back side of the rug canvas on a frame. Either leave the loops to vary the texture of the rug or cut them to be more like the tufted knots. The speed hooked sections should be latexed.

If you knot a piece of yarn unevenly so that one side is higher than the other, the shorter end of yarn will help the longer end to stay vertical. The shorter strand should be at least half the height of the longer strand. Uneven knotting is recommended for rugs with a pile higher than 2 inches. (A pile higher than 2 inches is impractical to walk on.) Knot the rows

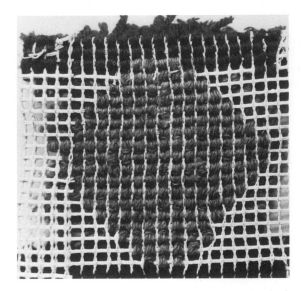

Fig. 10-11 (*above*) Back view of a latch hooked circle. Note the upper corner with the two edges hooked together. One edge is folded onto the front of the rug, the other onto the rug back, facilitating the double knotting.

Fig. 10-12 Front view of a latch hooked circle.

Plate 24 (*right*) "Two People Talking," 1966, a rug designed by the painter Robert Jay Wolfe. It was made with the latch hook technique.

so that the tall strand lies on alternate sides, to the right on even rows, to the left on uneven rows. This is better than having tall strands on only one side, although it could be done for a particular effect.

To test the density of the pile, and to see how it will stand and how clear the line definition will be, knot a small square and squeeze your fingers around it.

Some rugmakers, including Harley Jensen, use a frame to support the latch hooked rug while it is being worked on. He also uses 2- and 3-ply thin rug yarn (mill ends) and cuts it according to the method described on page 83. Figure 10-18 shows a rug in progress, with the design drawn on the backing. The rug has a 2¼-inch pile. You can see that by using thinner strands of yarn the effect is almost like fleece. Figure 19 shows Jensen's first rug. It is 34 by 58 inches and took five months of working in the evenings to complete. The mesh used in this rug has four holes to the inch.

Fig. 10-13 (*top*) Front view detail of a Steinberg woven tapestry, showing latch hook checkerboard method. Tapestry for Charles Slatkin galleries.

Fig. 10-14 Back view of the Steinberg detail.

Art Rugs

Many of the photographs in this chapter are from an exhibition called "Rugs" held at the Stephen Radich Gallery in New York in 1966. All the designs for rugs were especially created by painters, architects, and other artists for the latch hook technique. The show is reminiscent of the success of the Bauhaus where the object was to interest artists in designing utilitarian items.

The credit for this exhibition belongs to Leslie and Rufus Stillman. Two years before the show, in 1964, when they were having a new house designed by their friend Marcel Breuer, they asked another friend, Alexander Calder, to design a rug for the house. Calder drew the design of their first latch hooked rug directly on the rug canvas and Louisa Calder showed the Stillmans how to latch hook. The first rug has a raccoon, a sun, a moon, and a snake on a red background (fig. 10-18 and color plate 25).

The idea of a collection of latch hooked rugs designed by artists began to take shape. Fourteen artist-friends of the Stillmans and two other well-known painters designed rugs and each was given a rug with his own design in return. The Stephen Radich Gallery joined the effort and an exhibition of rugs was organized. The rugs were priced according to their size; the smallest sold for three hundred dollars, and the two largest, designed by John Johansen and Marcel Breuer, sold for fifteen hundred dollars each.

The rugs were displayed in the gallery in such a way that they could be walked on and seen from all angles. Consequently the workmanship could be properly inspected and appreciated. The rugs were made by Leslie Stillman, Gertrude Palmer, Margery Humphrey, and Elodie Osborn, who made two rugs that were designed by her husband and son.

One rug was designed by Constance Breuer, and Gertrude Palmer and Leslie Stillman worked on it together (fig. 10-17). From their

Fig. 10-15 (*top*)   Latch hooked rug (in progress) by Harley Jensen.

Fig. 10-16 (*center*)   Latch hooked rug (34″ × 58″) by Harley Jensen. Made of mill ends and with a 2½-inch pile, it took him five months to hook, working evenings, and cost him thirty dollars.

Fig. 10-17   Latch hooked rug designed by Constance Breuer and knotted in adjoining sections by Leslie Stillman and Gertrude Palmer.

Plate 25 Rug (5'6" × 6'9"), designed by Alexander Calder for Rufus and Leslie Stillman.

Fig. 10-18 Another view of Calder rug.

90

experience they don't recommend the making of a complex latch hooked rug with someone else because they had to proceed at an even rate in order to have all the lines of the design match.

Since this exhibition, Leslie Stillman has made many other latch hooked rugs. In the winter of 1973, the Stillmans began latch hooking rectangular bench rugs for their new house. Instead of having friends design the rugs, Rufus designed them.

It is a unique privilege to see rugs designed by artists who are proficient in other media. We see how they think of rugs as a medium of design and also how these designs relate to the artist's own work.

The yarn used in the above-mentioned rugs was purchased ready-dyed from Wm. Condon & Sons, Ltd. The pile was cut to a uniform height of 1¼ inches with the Bernat commercial cutter and knotted into the smaller size of four-to-an-inch rug canvas.

The geometric latch hooked rugs and wall hangings in color plates 32, 39 are the work of John Adolph of Oakland, California. He has been making latch hooked rugs for eighteen years from designs drawn in colored inks or watercolors on graph paper. He buys acrylic yarn and ties four strands together on the four-mesh rug canvas for an inch-high pile.

Traute Ishida follows a schedule of working four to five hours a day, including Saturdays and Sundays, on her latch hooked pieces. (See figs. 2-3, 4; 10-22–25; 12-4 and color plates 1, 4, 9, 27–31, 38.) In this way she is able to complete a large work in a few months. She began rugmaking with pre-cut yarn and has progressed to huge freeform wall hangings using a variety of materials. She told me the following: "I got my materials from Shillcraft. They of course carry kits but also sell packs of ready-cut wool and canvases on request. . . . The three holes to an inch I faithfully filled without skipping. I wanted at that time a tightly closed surface. I called my works 'floor pieces.' But eventually I became more and

Plate 26 "The Matador," latch hooked rug designed by Robert Osborn.

more involved with line and color modulation, also in changing the pile. I knotted plastic wrap, foil, newspaper, twigs, and grass into the canvas. I slit the canvas and wrapped it with unspun nylon. . . . Finally, I went to wool outlet stores and bought whatever struck my fancy, surrounding myself with loads of stuff, using and taking as my feeling and moods dictated—no longer striving for a carefully laid-out design and filling in the color-fields.

"It all happened gradually, the piece I was working on had grown out of the previous one, with my mind already on the following. Instead of hooking pieces of cut wool, I would loop strings into the canvas, skipping holes and rows. Anyway, they are no longer floor pieces.

It was a nice feeling to stand on them, but you can't really get a good view that way."

"Polar Ice" (fig. 10-26) is a wall hanging that was latch hooked with rayon, silk, and cotton yarn, and decorated with a glass bubble. It was made by an instructor of weaving, Helmi Moulton, at the University of Michigan in Kalamazoo. The backing for this piece is small-mesh rug canvas and the pile varies from 1 inch to 4 inches.

I hope that the latch hook technique catches up to other rug hooking techniques in popularity in the United States. Already, the number of advertisements by companies selling latch hook kits seems to indicate that latch hooking is becoming more and more popular.

Fig. 10-19 Latch hooked rug (56″ × 60″), designed by Norman Ives.

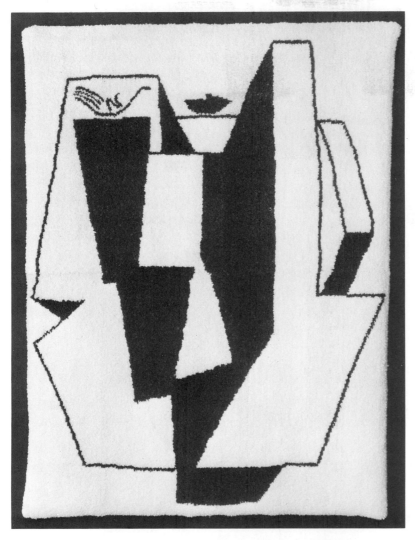

Fig. 10-20 (*top*) Latch hooked rug (60″ × 82″), designed by Constantino Nivolo, a sculptor, for Rufus and Leslie Stillman.

Fig. 10-21 Latch hooked rug, 1961 (42″ × 60″), designed by Carl Holty.

Plate 27 "On Vacation" (60″ × 87″), a latch hooked wall hanging by Traute Ishida.

Plate 28 "Nova Scotia," a latch hooked wall hanging by Traute Ishida.

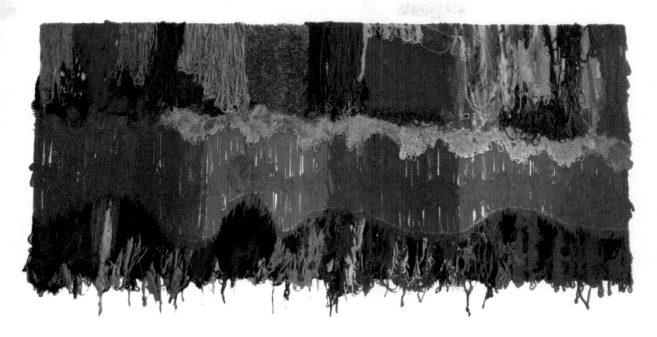

Plate 29 (*above*) "Rolling Stones" (115″ × 50″),
a latch hooked piece by Traute Ishida.

Plate 30 Detail of "Rolling Stones."

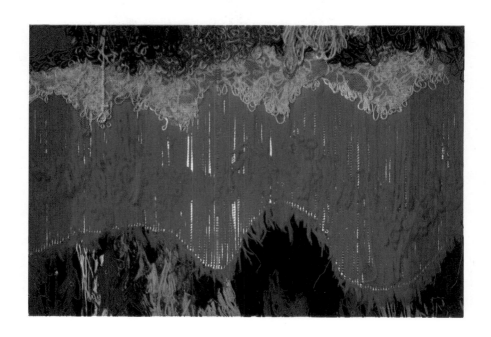

Fig. 10-22 (*above*) "Seeds" (10' × 8'), a latch hooked wall hanging by Traute Ishida.

Fig. 10-23 Latch hooked rug by Traute Ishida.

Fig. 10-24 Latch hooked wall hanging by Traute Ishida.

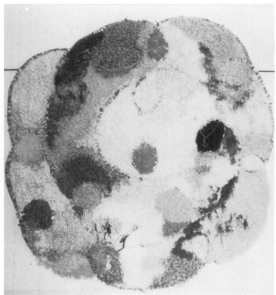

Fig. 10-25 Latch hooked wall hanging by Traute Ishida.

Fig. 10-26 ''Polar Ice'' (18″ × 40″), a latch hooked wall hanging by Helmi K. Moulton.

Plate 31 ''Guests Are Gone'' (60″ × 80″), a latch hooked wall hanging by Traute Ishida.

98

Plate 32 Latch hooked rug by John Adolph, knotted with three strands of acrylic yarn per knot.

11

The Rya

The Rya Today

The rya, or the shag rug, can be either woven or knotted and consequently appeals to more rugmakers.

The rya pile is unlike that of other rugs; a rya is a succession of fringes that cover a flat weave. Instead of the tops of yarn ends, you see the sides of the yarn.

According to Scandinavian authorities, the rya originated in the tenth century. The Scandinavians knotted pieces of wool into their woven blankets to create a fur-like effect. Ryas were first used on beds and put pile-side down for added warmth. In time, ryas were also hung on walls to keep out drafts. As the rya became a source of decoration, attention was devoted to color and design. Because of its popularity as a bedcover or wall hanging, the Scandinavian family incorporated the rya into their everyday weaving. An inch or so was woven in a flat tabby weave and then the next weft was pulled out through the warp threads to hang down as a fringe. The tabby weave holds the rya pile in place and the rya fringe gives texture, color, and all the other attributes of pile to the flat weave.

It might be only a coincidence, but in the tenth century when rya originated, Viking raids in the Mediterranean were at their height. It is more than likely that the Vikings brought back samples of hooked cloth with their plunder. It's interesting that the hooked technique did not catch on. A probable reason is that rya was already too firmly entrenched in the weaving technique of the North.

The nonwoven rya knot is an adaptation of the Ghiordes, or Turkish, knot in Oriental carpets, but the stylistic differences are enormous. The Ghiordes knot is not really a knot, but a fine strand of yarn wrapped around warp ends, cut to be miniscule and held in a row by one or two wefts. The rya knot is made of several strands of yarn tied securely between the warp ends. The long ends are left to hang.

Fig. 11-1 "Jungle" (23″ × 39″), a rya rug made on rya backing by Elizabeth Afkleen.

Fig. 11-2 "Shaped Rug I" (35″ × 60″) by Cynthia Schira. It was made with handspun Mexican wool yarn—a woven rya with a 1-inch pile.

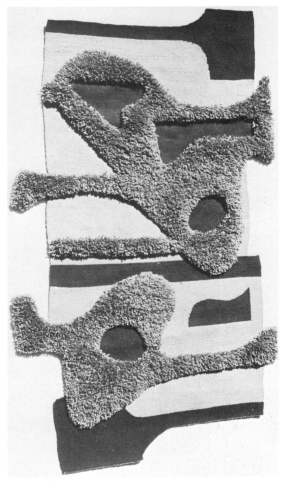

Fig. 11-3 "Shaped Tapestry II" (38" × 64"), a woven rya by Cynthia Schira.

The knotted rya has many advantages. For example, the rya knot will last a century. The backing is strong and does not need to be latexed. The knots are sewn in place on the rugmaker's lap. The rya is very light and portable, and can be rolled up when completed. It can easily be shaken out when it's dirty. It is warm enough to be used as a bedcover, light enough to be a wall hanging, and strong enough to be a long-lasting floor covering.

All good woven rya backing is imported from Scandinavia. The warp is made of linen for strength and the tabby weave in between the exposed warp is thick and soft. The backing is measured and cut according to the metric system, but in the United States it is sold by the yard in widths from 15½ inches to 6 feet 6 inches. It is also sold in special rug sizes for added convenience. One company offers twenty-one different sizes ranging from 2 feet by 3 feet to 6½ feet by 9 feet. Round ryas can be made in four sizes: the diameters of the backing measure 47, 59, 67, and 79 inches. The one oddity about metric dimensions is that there is no backing size between 32 and 39 inches. Aside from this, the backing is perfect and will keep the rya in condition for generations. A rya will last longer than any other pile rug.

As might be expected, rya backing (fig. 11-6) is very expensive. The average price is $1.75 per square foot. Its strength and promise of longevity should be worth this amount, but if not, there are alternatives.

Use rug warp or monk's cloth as your rya backing. It will not last as long as the regular rya backing, but it can be placed over a rug pad. Hem the sides ½ inch and make the first and last rya knot in every row through this double layer. To insure correct spacing, measure the first row in inches so you can make the right number of knots, and to make the rows straight, pull a pencil point along the weave of the cloth.

The other advantage, besides the difference in price, is that you can determine your own

Plate 33 (*left*) Rya pillow (2′ square), woven by Sarah Harkness.

Plate 34 Pillow (2′ square), designed and woven by Sarah Harkness.

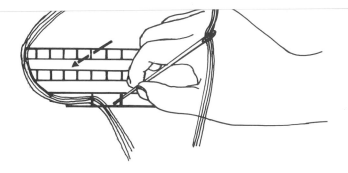

Plate 35 Rya pillow with a suede backing (2′ square), woven by Sarah Harkness.

103

hand corner of the backing. Pointing the needle upward, go under the left warp thread and pull the yarn up so there is an inch, or whatever pile length is desired, hanging down between the threads. This is the first part of the rya pile; hold it down with your thumb for the next step. To make the rya knot, bring the needle around clockwise above the warp threads; pointing the needle downward, put it under the right warp thread. Pull this knot tight and you have secured the rya pile. Leave a loop of yarn the same length as the first yarn ends and proceed to the next pair of warp threads. (See fig. 11-8.)

Fig. 11-8 Rya knot technique.

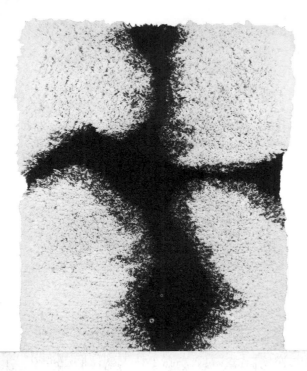

Fig. 11-4 (*top left*) "Fjord" (45" × 60"), a rya woven by Park Chambers. There is one tabby weave between each rya row, and the pile varies from ¼ inch to 4 inches. There are four rows to the inch.

Fig. 11-5 (*above*) Detail of "Fjord."

Fig. 11-6 (*bottom left*) Sample of rya backing cloth.

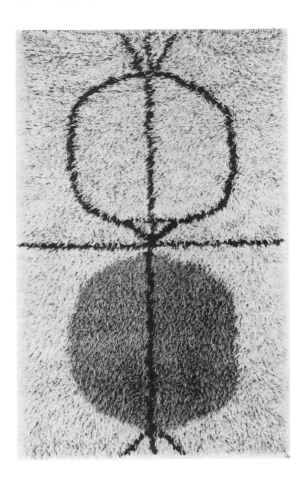

Fig. 11-9 (*above*) Rya rug kit pattern from Berga.

Fig. 11-10 Untitled woven rya (3' × 5') by Jack Arends.

The rya knot is actually an X with the cross as the base of the knot. If you are left-handed, begin in the lower right-hand corner. Push the needle under the right thread, go up and around the warp threads and back under the left warp thread. Pull tight and proceed.

If you hold the first fringe down, it will not shorten when you pull the rya knot. The loops can be cut at the end of the row. If you want to change colors before the yarn runs out, make the last knot and cut off the length of yarn equal to the other lengths of pile.

It is easiest to make the rya in rows progressing away from you. Rya pile should be just long enough to cover the knots in the preceding row. Adjust the length by leaving enough yarn between the warp threads and holding the yarn with your thumb while making the knot. There are gauges for exact measurements, but I don't believe it is necessary to buy one. A ruler can serve just as well; simply work the needle around it and the pile will be all of the same length.

The pile can be any length at all, but for practical purposes, a rya rug should have a pile from ½ inch to 2½ inches. Rugs cannot have a very long pile because it would be too easy for shoes to accidentally lift the pile up and expose the backing. Pillows can have a shorter pile. Loops of rya pile will be longer and lie flatter when they are cut. They can be cut evenly or unevenly for a shag effect, or some can be cut and some can be left in loops. The rounded loops are softer than the cut pile. Loops should not be left long enough to catch a shoe heel and cause an accident.

If the design has many colors, buy several rya needles or blunt-tipped tapestry needles. Thread them with the different colors you are using and keep them in a pin cushion near you. Lines and spots of contrasting colors are made by sewing individual knots throughout the rya; lines and spots should be done as you come to them in each row or you may find it difficult locating each spot when the whole rya has been knotted.

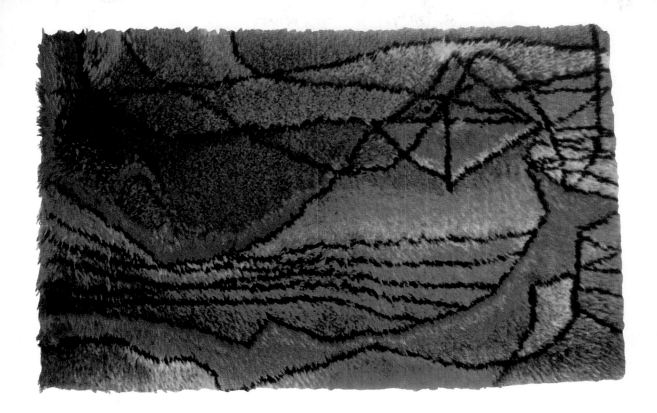

Plate 36 (*top*)   Untitled woven rya (3′ × 5′) by Jack Arends. There are two to four rows and six to eight knots per inch.

Fig. 11-11   Untitled woven rya (3′ × 5′) by **Jack Arends.**

Fig. 11-12 (*top*) "Falling Leaves" (45″ × 76″), a woven rya by Sarah Harkness. The rya pile is 1¾ inches long.

Fig. 11-13 "Oil Slick," a hand-knotted rya pillow by Marie Berler.

A fringe at either end of the rya can be made by tying the same rya knot, but you must lengthen the pile. Or you can differentiate the fringe from the rya by skipping every other pair of threads and using less yarn. The fringe should be in proportion to the rya and never exceed 5 inches, or it will be too long to keep straight.

Rya backings in special sizes are hemmed and ready to use. Backings sold by the yard require a hem, which can be very narrow—½ inch is sufficient even for large rugs—but it should be sewn before the rya is begun. The rug is light and relatively flat and therefore needs no further binding. Sections of ryas that have been finished individually can be joined by overcast stitches along the backs of the rya.

The tuft of a rya knot is actually a triangle, the small end being the knot, the larger elongated part the pile. It is much broader in comparison with the pile of other rugmaking techniques and therefore the design has to be less detailed. When the loops are cut unevenly, there is a more ripply effect than when they are cut straight or left as is. The pile can also be varied if more yarn is used in some places or if a combination of thinner rya yarn is mixed with thicker yarn. As many as five strands can be used, although usually three are used. If the density of the pile is altered by adding strands, texture and color variation is more spectacular.

Although the colors, texture, and length of pile may be changed, the direction of rya pile is constant. It all lies in one definite direction, like ridges. The rya can go against the design, but it usually goes with it. The spacing of the knots is another constant. Some backings, such as the Borg, accommodate four knots to the inch, but there are usually only three.

The distance between the rows of rya knots can be considerable. The rows of a rya backing are spaced ½ inch apart. A rya with a pile of slightly more than an inch is knotted in every other row; a Greenland rya, which has a 2½-inch pile, is knotted in every fourth row.

When the rows are closer together and the pile short, greater clarity of line and consequently of pattern detail is possible.

Lines of a design are emphasized by changing the length of the pile. In "Lineal Descendant II" (fig. 11-14), Marie Berler used black lines of 1-inch pile to divide the colors knotted with 3-inch pile. Varying the length of pile clarifies the lines.

The spacing of the rya knots does not alter the amount of yarn used in the rug, wall hanging, or pillow. But the time spent on the rya is lessened if the pile is long. An average rya with a pile of an inch takes approximately three hours a square foot at the rate of five knots a minute. With fewer knots and a longer pile, a Greenland rya could be completed in half the time of a shorter-pile rya.

The work time just mentioned for the rya does not take into account any time spent deciding on colors or changing the pattern. The virtue of a rya is that even though it can be made quickly, the pleasure is in its color blendings and design. Combinations take more time, but they make a better-looking rya.

A store in Manhattan once displayed a rya rug in its window that had many different reds in it, no other colors, and no design. The effect was appreciated by hundreds of people, and the manager of the store still speaks of this rug's popularity.

Beautiful color combinations can be achieved with a rya. There are so many colors available, the rya rugmaker can be adventuresome about gradations of color and shades. Traditionally ryas have dealt with subtle color changes and have used abstract designs to fully explore color. When you are working on the rya, you will be more aware of the finer color contrasts than the viewer looking at the finished rug. To you the thin strands of yellow and blue may look distinct, but to the viewer five feet away, fine yellow and blue lines will look green and fine red and green lines will look brown. The eye naturally blends these colors together. Remember that!

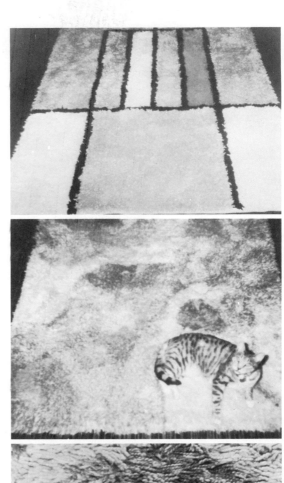

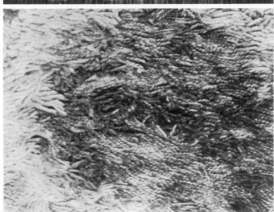

Fig. 11-14 (*top*) "Lineal Descendant II" (5′ × 8′) by Marie Berler. This rya, sewn on backing material, has four knots to the inch, and there are 2½ rows per inch.

Fig. 11-15 (*center*) "Carrara Clouds," a rya knotted rug by Marie Berler.

Fig. 11-16 Detail of the texture of "Carrara Clouds."

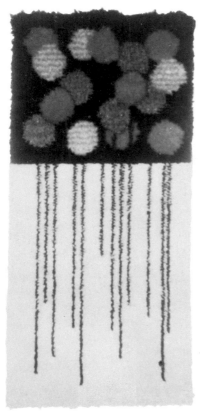

Fig. 11-17 (*top*)   "Mother Nacre" (18" × 24"), a wall hanging by Marie Berler. The background is in a reverse diagonal tent stitch; the shell is tufted rya knots.

Fig. 11-18   Rya hand-knotted rug by Marie Berler.

As with latch hooked rugs, shapes in ryas are made by increasing and decreasing the number of knots in the rows. The shorter the curve and the longer the pile, the more difficult it is to reproduce the shape.

A circle would be represented in steps on a graph paper design of a rya pattern. Special rya graph paper is blocked off into 3-inch squares; nine knots and seven rows can be represented in each square. Regular graph paper can also be used. For "Matisse Branches" (fig. 11-21), 36 inches by 60 inches, Marie Berler made a large oaktag stencil and traced the outlines onto the backing. She wanted to preserve the hard edge of the branches so she spaced the rows two and one-half to the inch and the knots four to the inch. Her other ryas are knotted from a sketch a third the size of the finished rug.

Weavers often make a sketch and put it behind their looms so they can follow it easily. Cynthia Schira, trained to be a tapestry weaver in Aubusson, France, where the design is of utmost importance, said that if a student's sample differed so much as an eighth of an inch from the cartoon, the weaving was ripped out and had to be done again. Many rugmakers, however, start off with a general idea of a pattern and as they work, the forms and design are developed by the colors.

Another rya weaver, Sarah Harkness, uses a pantograph to enlarge her rug patterns. (See color plates 33–35, fig. 11-22.) You can, however, draw lines directly onto the backing with an indelible felt-tip marker. To make a more exact rendition of the color combinations of the design, you can note the colors of the knots above every row. You can devise a color code so that you will know exactly how much yarn will be required. Directions for color coding are given on page 22.

The rya technique can be used to decorate clothes. In "Chevron Shirt" (fig. 11-23) and "Chaps" (fig. 11-24) Carole Lubove has done what Scandinavian rya makers have also begun to do. "Chevron Shirt" was made with a sideways "Persian" knot instead of the Ghiordes because the pile had to lie in another direction. For the Persian knot, the yarn goes over the first warp thread, under and back around over the second, and out under the first thread. The pile is from 4 to 5 inches high, with one row of knots every ⅝ inch and either four or five strands of yarn in every pile row.

Rya is the one rugmaking technique particularly appropriate to clothes.

There are several companies that sell rya kits for pillows, wall hangings and rugs at very reasonable prices. The kits include the backing, wool yarn, needles, and pile gauge. Some rugs are pre-started; some wall hangings come with rings and rods for hanging the work. The designs are all created by Scandinavian artists and are reproduced well in the color plates of the various catalogs. The only drawback is that instructions for these designs are in the same difficult format as knitting directions.

It is a good idea to look at the designs offered by these companies even if you are going to make your own design. From them you can learn a great deal about color and variety of design, and they are very good for commercial kits.

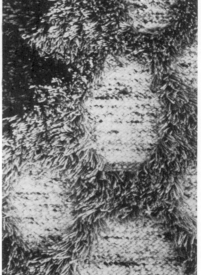

Fig. 11-19 (*above*) Woven rya rug by Helmi K. Moulton.

Fig. 11-20 Detail of woven rya by Helmi K. Moulton.

Fig. 11-21 "Matisse Branches," a knotted rya rug by Marie Berler.

Fig. 11-22 Rya rug woven by Sarah Harkness.

Plate 37 Detail of rya rug woven by Sarah Harkness.

Fig. 11-23 (*above*) Rya shirt, woven by Carole Lubove.

Fig. 11-24 "Chaps" by Carole Lubove. A tubular weave rya, it has one knot per inch, five to six strands of yarn to each knot, and a 3- to 4-inch pile.

12

Dyeing Yarn and Materials

I have found that the all-purpose dyes that are commonly recommended for rugmaking are inferior to dyes made for a particular fiber. The disadvantage in using such dyes (for example, Cushing Perfection dyes and Putnam's Fadeless dyes) is that they contain different coloring agents for the various fibers, and when you have dyed some wool, you have to rinse out the unused agents intended for other fabrics. However, these dyes are popular because they offer a wide range of subtle and blended colors.

For wool yarn and material, I use Craftsman's dyes, which are sold at The Ruggery, Glen Head, New York. One small package dyes 1½ pounds of white wool to full-color strength. Wool has proved colorfast in tests of full sunlight for three months (except for turquoise, which faded badly, and brown, which faded some). These dyes are used exclusively for wool and are the same dyes used in industry. Craftsman's dyes are available in eleven colors: red, yellow, blue, green, orange, violet, magenta, turquoise, blue-green, brown, and black. The dyes are easy to mix if you want a particular color. For convenience, The Ruggery also sells a wool yarn that has been treated to take these dyes in scalding hot tap water. The yarn is trademarked Meriwell Acidified yarn and is comparable in price to other domestic wool yarns that don't have this additional feature. The yarn can be re-dyed until the perfect shade is achieved.

Cotton, silk, and linen can be dyed permanently in cold-water reactive dyes. These recently developed dyes are available in basic colors. Cold-water dyeing produces brilliant colors with very little effort. Each package dyes 1 pound or 3 square yards to pastel shades.

Synthetic yarns and materials cannot be dyed at home because the dyes cannot penetrate the fabric because of its finish. Some dyes, however, can tint the fabric to another shade.

Chemical dyes were discovered in the middle of the nineteenth century. In 1856, eighteen-year-old Henry Perkin accidentally discovered mauve when he was trying to synthesize quinine from coal.

In ancient times people who made dyes handed down their recipes from generation to generation. In some parts of the world today, this is still done. In Renaissance Greece there were two thousand Jewish dyers distilling insects and herbs for the reds and yellows in Oriental carpets. To obtain blue they used the indigo plant which is not water-soluble. When they put yarn into a vat of dye collected from indigo plants, they could not see the color develop. Their practice was to add honey and raisins, dates, and other fruits to the vat. They allowed the fruits to ferment rapidly and added alkali. Then the indigo turned white. After a day or two the yarn was taken out of the vat, and when it was exposed to the air, it turned blue. Indigo is now available in water-soluble

Fig. 12-1 Dyeing a skein of yarn in a spaghetti pot with special wool dyes.

crystals and can be bought at organic herb stores that stock natural dyes.

There are many reasons for you to dye your own yarn, and if you are using material, dyeing becomes almost obligatory. Undyed yarn is cheaper to buy than dyed yarn, but all yarn is sold in quantity—the smallest amount, ¼ pound, can cover a square foot. If you want a special color, then you must either dye it yourself or plan to stock a lot of extra colors. Commercially dyed yarn, evenly penetrated with dye, produces one solid color. Home-dyed yarn, on the other hand, can be mottled and variegated, so that with wear and under different lighting it is richer-looking. The color can also be controlled by mixing dyes and by removing the material from the dye bath. Dyeing is creative and fun to do. Some rughookers prefer it to the actual rugmaking.

Some Hints on Dyeing

Material must be cleaned before it is dyed and should not be cut into strips, otherwise the edges will fray and the pieces will get tangled. The color can be removed from cloth by boiling it in strong soap flakes, or by using a commercial color remover, or washing with bleach. Lighter colors are easier to remove. When you bleach a color out, keep the material or yarn moving so that some areas will not be bleached more than others. Barbara Zarbock, author of *The Complete Book of Rug Hooking,* cautions that bleach will not work when the amount of color that has been removed from the fabric is equal to what is left. Therefore change the water frequently. Black is impossible to remove completely.

Wear an apron because dyes can stain your clothes indelibly. They will not stain porcelain, enamel, or other nonporous surfaces. To protect plastic and wood surfaces, cover them with newspapers.

A spaghetti pot, a pressure cooker, a large saucepan, or a roasting dish, preferably white

Fig. 12-2 Shuttle hooked and punch needle wall hanging by Shirley Marein.

enamel, can be used for dyeing. Cold-water dyes and Craftsman's wool dyes can be used with acidified yarn in the sink.

Pint-size glass jars with screw-on tops allow for mixing and storing the dye solutions.

Metal tongs or disposable sticks are required for stirring the yarn and material while it is being dyed. Rubber gloves protect the hands from hot water when the dyed goods are lifted from the dye bath. To measure the dyes, use metal measuring spoons.

You may want to keep a notebook for your recipes, and also keep color samples to provide you with an example of a particular dye. You can also make comparisons with other colors to be used in the rug.

The Dyeing Process

Fibers absorb dye through the water and with the help of a catalyst, the mordant, which is usually un-iodized salt or vinegar. The heat seals the dye into the wool fibers to make the dye colorfast. Cotton, linen, silk, nonacetate rayon, leather, sisal, and jute, which can all be dyed in cold water, require only a "fixer" of washing soda to bind the dye to the cloth. The temperature necessary for dyeing wool is between 180° F. and 220° F. Water boils at 212° F. at sea level and the boiling point decreases 1° F. for every five hundred feet of elevation. It does not matter if the yarn or fabric is boiled as long as the temperature of the water is changed gradually. If the fibers are plunged into boiling water or if after having boiled they are put immediately into cold water, the wool will shrink and the setting action of the dye will be upset. Therefore one important rule of dyeing wool or fibers is to always let the material heat and cool slowly.

The first time you dye wool, choose one color and one pound of yarn or material. Untwist the skeins of yarn and, with short pieces of yarn, tie the loose strands in three places. This will prevent the yarn from getting twisted and

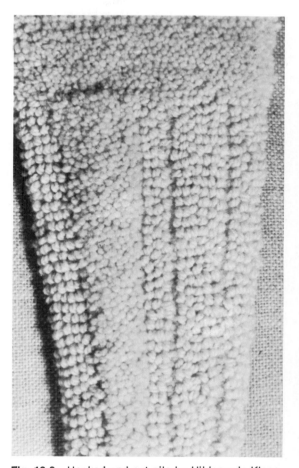

Fig. 12-3   Hooked and cut pile by Hildegarde Klene.

tangled in the water. Fill a pot with a gallon of warm water (add water softener to hard water) and put the pot on the stove over medium heat. Put in half a cup of white vinegar or un-iodized salt as the mordant.

Empty one package of dye into a glass jar and add the amount of water specified on the package. Shake the jar and when the dye is dissolved, pour it into the dye water.

Wet the yarn before dyeing it so that the dye will take more evenly. Soak the yarn in the sink a few minutes or hold it under lukewarm tap water and then put it into the dye bath. Lift the yarn or material up and turn it periodically so that all of it gets dyed. As the water heats, the dye is absorbed and the fibers turn the color of the dye solution. Any color when wet looks darker, and when it is concentrated in a mass, it tends to look brighter. To test for the color you want, take a strand and rub it dry between your fingers. This is the shade the yarn will be if you take it out of the dye water at that moment. The rate of the dye's absorption and the depth of color depend on several factors: the length of time the yarn or material is in the dye bath, the amount of water, and the heat. The amount of material in the pot and the quantity of water in proportion to the dye control the rate of the dyeing process. If you use Craftsman's dyes correctly, the dye water will become clear when all the dye is absorbed.

If the material reaches the right color before all the dye is absorbed, take the material out of the pot and pour out the water. Fill the pot

Fig. 12-4   Latch hooked rug by Traute Ishida.

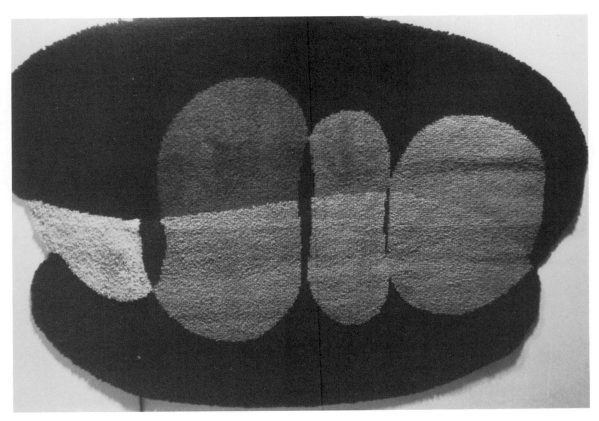

with scalding hot water and return the dyed material to the pot. Darker colors that have been simmering on the stove for more than a half hour are sure to have set and are ready to cool. Light colors should be steamed. This is accomplished by pouring off most of the water, covering the pot, and putting it in a 350° F oven for fifteen minutes. The intense heat in the pot will assure the setting of the color. You should also do this if you are not sure the dye has taken. It would be a great shame to dye the colors and then find when you first wash the rug that they are not colorfast.

Excess water can be shaken or wrung out of the dyed material. It should then be hung either inside or outside to dry. Don't use an automatic dryer, however. The yarn will become tangled, and intense heat and tumbling are not good for fibers soon to be hooked or knotted into a rug.

You can dye over other dyed yarns for extra deep color. Dye both natural light yarns and white for a blend of colors. Shades that are closely related will remain consistent when they are dyed together. For example, if pink and yellow are both dyed blue, the resulting colors will be similar shades of green and purple. The more colors that are mixed together, the darker the dye water becomes and hence the material. If you want a single color to be darker, add some of the dye solution of its complementary color instead of brown or black. For example, to darken red, add green dye.

Dry yarn or material put directly into a dye bath will color unevenly. You may want to take advantage of this for a particular effect. Also the yarn and material can be tie-dyed, that is, tightly fastening parts of the material so the dye won't color those places. An eyedropper can be used to make stripes and patterns on the skeins. Strips of material can be brushed with a paintbrush dipped in dye solution and then the color set by steaming the material in the oven. Mixing colors directly in the dye bath is a bold action. Until you are experienced you

should practice with a small quantity of dye and material in a small saucepan.

The length of time the yarn or material is in the dye bath determines the color. The longer it is submerged, the darker the color. For good color gradation either add more material to the dye bath every few minutes or put all the material into the pot and remove portions as the dye is absorbed.

To dye a large quantity of material or yarn, use a large enamel bathtub and mix all of the dye solution first, then divide it up for successive dye baths. When each bath is finished, drain the water out, and begin anew. Small amounts of material can be dyed in a small saucepan or bread pan with a few inches of water. The dye solution is sprinkled on the material, which is then steamed in the oven. This will create a mottled effect.

Fig. 12-5 Detail of "Pittsburgh" by Hildegarde Klene, hooked with a punch needle. After a drawing by José Bermudez.

If you are planning to use the dye water for more yarn or material, set the material to be dyed in a pot of simmering water. When its temperature is the same as the dye bath, move the dyed material into the plain hot water and the new material into the dye bath.

In Guatemala the weavers of Lake Atitlán have an interesting method of dyeing a skein of yarn in two colors. The yarn is wrapped around a board and half is immersed in the dye bath. After this half has dried, the other half is dyed in a different dye bath.

Professional dyers mix dyes like watercolors. I recommend that the beginner practice with small quantities. A little dark dye goes a very long way in a light dye bath and too much of a color's complement will turn the solution dark gray. If you are mixing colors and forget what primary colors you are using, Catherine Eichelberger of the Cornell Home Extension Service advises blowing a few drops of the dye onto a paper towel and the individual blue, red, and yellow will "pop out." When you are mixing dyes, be careful to wash the spoon before you put it into another dye solution because the dye will carry and the colors will change accordingly. However, don't be too concerned about imperfections in the dyeing process—imperfections can look pleasing in the rug or wall hanging.

Plate 38   Latch hooked wall hanging by Traute Ishida.

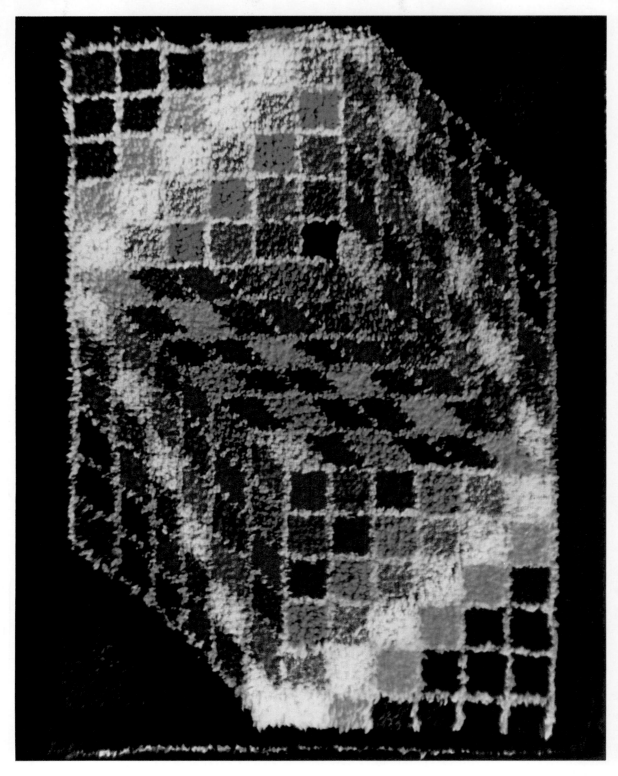

Plate 39 Latch hooked rug by John Adolph, made with acrylic yarn.

Afterword

The rugmaking techniques described in this book can be combined. Shirley Marein used both a Tru-Gyde and a Columbia Minerva punch needle in some works. The photograph of the eyes peering out in the wall hanging add another special touch to the work (fig. A-1).

The detail of "Meadow Flowers" (fig. A-2) contrasts Helmi K. Moulton's weaving with the texture of wood. She says: "Often I use wood in my weavings. Wood has such beauty in its grain and coloring. In this piece I gouged and drilled it for texture, painted it chartreuse, and applied gold leaf." The appliqué, rya, and machine stitched rug, "Desert Flower" (figs. A-6, A-7) was also made by Ms. Moulton. The rya pile is in rows ½ inch apart. The detail demonstrates the effect she wanted to achieve.

The extremely long pile rugs of Yvonne Bobrowicz include fleece (fig. A-3). The rya is woven; the pile is from 2 to 10 inches long and the rows are 1 inch apart. She also uses feathers, copper wire, and fur in her work for a more sculptural, three-dimensional effect.

"Linear Face," a wall hanging, was woven by Evelyn Anselevicius (figs. A-4, A-5). It is a masterpiece. From a distance it looks like a gigantic photograph of a girl's face, but close up, or from the side, the "face" is not to be seen. The white and black background was woven on a 79-inch Mexican serape loom. All of the yarn is Mexican handspun wool; the black was dyed with Ciba-Geigy Mexicana dyes.

Ms. Anselevicius studied at Black Mountain with Josef Albers and with Buckminster Fuller at the Design Institute in Chicago. She has lived and worked in India and in Bolivia, and now lives in San Miguel de Allende, Mexico.

In "Linear Face," rough sketches of thin and thick lines were drawn in India ink but were not enlarged, nor was the design transferred to the warp. "Linear Face" was woven in 1½-inch white bands between three rows of black stripes. The tufts of black pile were pulled up with a rug hook to make the face. The height of the pile varies from 0 to 1½ inches. The final touches to this work were added when the hanging was removed from the loom and hung for a period of three months. During that time, Ms. Anselevicius altered, trimmed, and added to the pile.

Concerning "Linear Face," she wrote: "This

Fig. A-1 Detail of "A Place Called Golgotha," shuttle hooked and punch needle hooked by Shirley Marein.

kind of thing cannot be done effectively in bright colors. Only colors with the endurance of stone are capable of rendering the timeless serenity required." But she believes a work like this could be done on a cloth backing with the rug hooking techniques discussed in this book. She has also said that "large-scale weaving ought to be entered into with an attitude similar to that of a sculptor working in stone," and that "something [is] lost when structure becomes texture." These two quotations were responses to questions asked her by Mildred Constantine in connection with a book entitled *Beyond Craft: The Art Fabric.*

The mixture of weaving, pile knotting, and hooking cannot yet be fully explored because there are relatively few craftsmen who combine the flat and pile techniques. Those who do,

however, keep experimenting with different tools and mediums. The contrast between the flat weave and a knotted or hooked pile is a very basic one, but one open to unlimited possibilities.

The principal difference between a woven rug and a pile rug is that a woven rug is made on a loom by interlacing strands of yarn or material, and the shape of the finished rug is almost always square or rectangular. A pile rug can be made either with or without a frame, the design can be anything at all, and the height of the pile can be varied. The size, shape, and dimensions of the rug are all flexible.

I hope that these flexible properties of pile rugs will be explored fully someday.

Fig. A-2   Detail of "Meadow Flowers" (20″ × 36″), wool and wood hanging by Helmi K. Moulton.

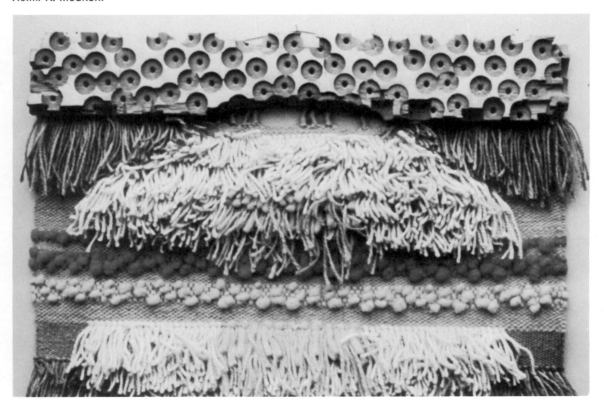

Fig. A-3 Detail of a rya rug woven with fleece by Yvonne Bobrowicz.

Fig. A-4 "Linear Face" (77" × 84"), side view. It was woven by Evelyn Anselevicius on a Mexican serape loom and has a hand hooked pile.

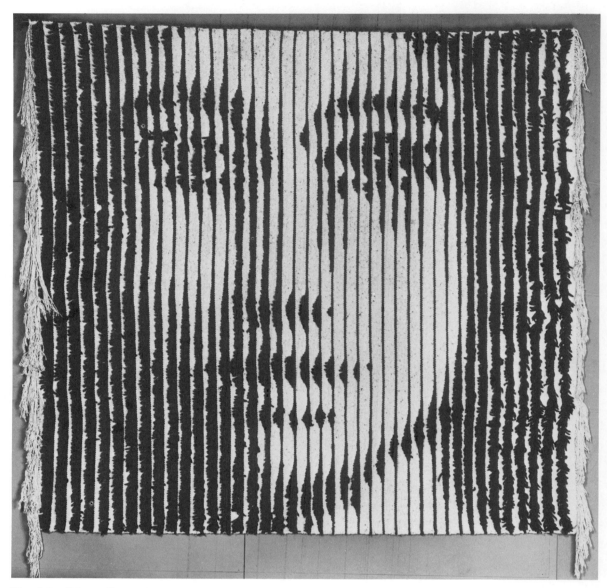

Fig. A-5 "Linear Face," front view.

Fig. A-6 (*above*) "Desert **Flower**" (2′ × 3′), appliqué and machine stitched **woven** rya wall hanging by Helmi K. Moulton.

Fig. A-7   Detail of "Desert Flower."

APPENDIX I: Rug Cleaning and Care

I learned an infallible method for rug cleaning in Blue Hill, Maine, that you might want to try if you live in snow country. Place the rug, pile-side down, on the snow. Do this on a cold sunny day. This gets the rug clean, it smells fresh, and there is no work for you. This works especially well on nonlatexed rugs.

Sweep up crumbs and dust from a rug before they get ground in. Ground-in dirt is harder to remove, though a vacuum cleaner is usually effective. A periodic shaking out of the rug and turning it to equalize wear will help the appearance of a rug. Whenever possible, try to put the rug where it is likely to be walked on with slippers or barefeet as opposed to shoes, to help maintain its luster, longevity, and cleanliness.

Stains are a nuisance, especially on rugs. Scotchgard is excellent protection against stains, but you may want to try one of the following home remedies if a rug gets stained. Before you prepare the cleanser, first blot the stain with paper towels and salt or baking soda.

Cleansers

1 tsp. of soft dishwashing detergent
  (no soap, no bleach)
1 qt. of water and 1 tsp. of vinegar to neutralize any alkali

or

1/3 cup of white vinegar
2/3 cup of warm water

or

1 tbsp. of household ammonia
3/4 cup of warm water
  (This is especially good to brighten colors.)

Moisten the paper towel and work from the edge of the stain to the center. As the moisture evaporates, the stain will transfer to the blotter. If the first attempt fails, try again with a different solution.

If a cigarette ash burns wool pile, the residue can be removed with sandpaper. If a cigarette ash burns synthetic pile, the scar must be cut off. Grease and gum stains should be removed with a dry-cleaning fluid if the detergent-vinegar solution fails.

It should be noted that dry-cleaning fluids don't work well on cotton pile and must be used sparingly on latex-backed rugs. If you do use a strong cleanser, test a few drops on an inconspicuous part of the rug and cover it with a paper towel. If no color has been transferred to the towel after ten seconds, it is safe to use this cleanser.

Eventually a rug must be washed completely. There are two methods: dry cleaning and wet cleaning. A dry cleanser eliminates the danger of overwetting a rug. It is also faster. Dry-cleaning compounds are made of absorbent powders, sometimes a fine grain sawdust saturated with fat solvents. The absorbed dirt can then be vacuumed away. Special applicators are convenient, but not essential.

Washing a rug may take more time, but it can do a better cleaning job. Soap should not be used because it leaves a sticky film that will attract new dirt. It is also harder to rinse than a detergent. A dishwashing or gentle fabric detergent is desirable for wool and finely colored rugs that must be treated carefully. A good shampoo can be made in a blender by mixing ¼ cup of dishwashing detergent and one cup of warm water. Blend the solution until it is stiff and foamy.

A brush is better than a sponge because the bristles can reach farther. Spread a glob of shampoo on the rug. Scrub in a circular motion. The rug should feel damp, *never wet.* Remove the excess foam and rinse immediately. Apply more shampoo to an overlapping area and proceed as before.

Furniture legs can permanently stain a wet rug. Protect your rug by putting a piece of cardboard under furniture legs until you are sure the rug is dry. The rug will dry best on a dry windy day. Open the windows if you cannot air the rug outdoors.

Steaming can restore any crushed pile to its original height. Set your iron for wool. Moisten the area to be worked on, cover it with a dry cloth, and put the iron on the cloth. Press down for about ten seconds, or until the escape of steam has almost stopped. Brush up the pile.

A pad under a rug keeps it in place and protects the vulnerable backing. The traditional rug pad is made of mothproofed, sterilized, felted cattle hair, noted for its impact resistance. Now, however, latex and sponge backings are more popular. The ingredients are nonallergenic and are not affected by humidity or mildew. Embossed sponge pads are available in many thicknesses and can be cut to any size. Latex rubber is formed into sheets from a liquid mix, while sponge is filled with air cells. Clay and other inert ingredients are added to sponge and rubber as a filler. This often contributes to the decomposition of the mat. Compare the percentages of filler. The lower the percentage, the better the pad.

APPENDIX II:

List of Recommended Suppliers

Contessa Yarns
Lebanon, Conn. 06249
  various novelty yarns

Fraser Studio
192 Hartford Rd.
Manchester, Conn. 06040
  frames; backings; rug hooks;
  cutters; lacing sets; patterns,
  25¢; catalog

W. Cushing & Co.
Dover-Foxcroft, Me. 04426
  Cushing Perfection dyes, 94
  colors

Earth Guild, Inc.
149 Putnam Ave.
Cambridge, Mass. 02139

Woolcraft, Inc.
P.O. Box 747
Islington, Mass. 02090
  6-ply rug yarn packs and skeins,
  kits, 70 colors; rug canvas by
  the yd., 13 widths

Braid Aid
466 Washington St.
Pembroke, Mass. 02359
  frames; backings; hooks; dyes;
  cutters; lacing sets; samples,
  25¢

Persian Patterns
Pearl McGown, Inc.
West Boylston, Mass. 01583
  patterns, $3.50; catalog

Peters Valley Craftsmen
Peters Valley
Layton, N.J. 07851

Brooklyn Botanical Garden
1000 Washington Ave.
Brooklyn, N.Y. 11225
  dye plants and handbook, $1.25

The Ruggery
Glen Head, N.Y. 11545
  Craftsman's dyes; monk's cloth;
  rug hooks; 3-ply Meriwell
  acidified yarns

Coulter Studios
138 East 60 St.
New York, N.Y. 10804
  patterns; Borg yarns; backings;
  kits

School Products, Inc.
312 East 23 St.
New York, N.Y. 10010
  CUM yarns; supplies

George Barberean, Inc.
245 Fifth Ave.
New York, N.Y. 10016
  Persian wool rug yarn

John J. Ullman-Berga
Box 831
Ossining, N.Y. 10562
  Berga rya yarns; backings

The Mannings Creative Craft
East Berlin, Pa. 17316
  selected yarn lots; handspun;
  backings

House of Kleen
Canonchet Rd.,
Hope Valley, R.I. 02832
  Berga yarns, over 370 colors;

26 sizes rya backings; patterns,
$1.50

Craft Yarns of Rhode Island
P.O. Box 385
Pawtucket, R.I. 02862
  25¢ for a sample card of yarns

Heirloom Rugs
28 Harlem St.
Rumford, R.I. 02916
  400-plus hooked rug patterns,
  $1.00; catalog

Joyce L. Wilson
Rt. 2, Box 359
Dalton, Ga. 30720
  wool rug yarns

Lee Wards
Elgin, Ill. 60120
  scrim, all rug hooks

The Jacobsons
2524 Asbury Ave.
Evanston, Ill. 60201
  Berga yarns; backings

Norden Products
Glenview, Ill. 60025
  "Eggbeater" rug and rya
  yarns; latex; backings

Putnam, Inc.
Quincy, Ill. 62301
  Putnam-Fadeless dyes, 34
  colors

Countryside Handweavers
Box 1225
Mission, Kans. 61222
  yarns; Ciba dyes

Davidson's Old Mill Yarn
P.O. Box 115
Eaton Rapids, Mich. 48827
    wool, blends, acrylic yarns;
    rya; rug canvas; hooks; dis-
    counts on quantity orders;
    samples, $1.00

Wilson Brothers
Rt. 8, Box 3–H
Springfield, Mo. 65804
    Tru-Gyde; patterns; backings

Scandinavian Art Handicraft
7696 Camargo Rd.
Madeira, Cincinnati, Ohio 45243
    backings; yarns

Some Place
2990 Adeline St.
Berkeley, Calif. 94703
    yarn mill ends; wool, cotton,
    nylon dyes; frames; hooks;
    backings; cutters

Dharma Trading Co.
P.O. Box 1288
Berkeley, Calif. 94701

Meriskeins/Sharon Murfin
1741 Allston Way
Berkeley, Calif. 94703
    Mexican handspun yarn

The Yarn Loft
Box 771
Del Mar, Calif. 92014

The Yarn Depot
545 Sutter St.
San Francisco, Calif. 94102
    wool, cotton, silk yarns

Fibrec, Inc.
Box 14127
San Francisco, Calif. 94114
    permanent cold-water reactive
    dyes

Rug Crafters
1301 E. Edinger Bldg.
Santa Ana, Calif. 92705
    Speed Tufting Tool; latex;
    polyester yarns; backings;
    patterns

MarVar
P.O. Box 774
West Covina, Calif. 91790
    acrylic yarns

Greentree Ranch Wools
Box 461
Loveland, Colo. 80357

D'Kor Electric Needle
P.O. Box 1848
Carson City, Nev. 89701

Black Sheep Weaving and Craft
Supply
318 SW Second
Corvallis, Ore. 97330
    CUM yarns

Mayatex
P.O. Box 4452
El Paso, Tex.
    Mexican handspun

Intertwine
1121 Second Ave.
Salt Lake City, Utah
    CUM yarns

Wide World of Herbs, Ltd.
11 St. Catherine St. East
Montreal 129, Canada
    natural dyes and mordants

Rittermere Craft Studio
Box 240
Vineland, Ont., Canada
    patterns, $1.00

Briggs & Little Woolen Mill, Ltd.
York Mills
Harvey Station, N.B., Canada
    6-ply rug yarns, 24 colors;
    discount on more than 50 lbs.

Wm. Condon & Sons, Ltd.
P.O. Box 129
Charlottetown P.E.I., Canada
    5-ply run yarns, 38 colors;
    discount on more than 20 lbs.

Stavros Kouyoumoutzakis
Kalokerinou Ave. 166
Iraklion, Crete, Greece
    natural homespun wool

Lucan Yarn Mills
Lucan, Ireland
    6-ply rug yarn

Cambridge Wools, Ltd.
16–22 Anzac Ave.
Auckland, New Zealand
    thin rug yarn, natural colors

Bibliography

Allen, Edith L. *Rugmaking Craft.* Manual Arts Press, 1946.

Aller, Doris. *Rugs.* Sunset Books,

Berkeley, Bernard. "Selection and Maintenance of Commercial Carpet." Carpet and Rug Institute (Dalton, Ga.), 1970.

Constantine, Mildred, and Larsen, Jack Lenor. *Beyond Craft: The Art Fabric.* Reinhold, 1973.

Counts, Charles. "Encouraging American Craftsmen: Report of the Interagency Crafts Committee." Government Printing Office, 1971. (Stock #3600–0010, 45¢.)

Eichelberger, Catherine U. "Hooked Rugs." Cornell Miscellaneous Bulletin 43. New York State College of Home Economics, 1962.

Itten, Johannes. *Design and Form: The Basic Course at the Bauhaus.*

———. *The Art of Color.* Van Nostrand, 1970.

Jorges, Janet. "From Tough Times to Tufting." University of Tennessee. Thesis. 1971.

Kent, W. W. *The Hooked Rug.* Dodd, Mead, 1930.

Laury, Jean Ray, and Aiken, Joyce. *Handmade Rugs from Practically Anything.* Countryside Press, Farm Journal Inc., 1971. (Distributed by Doubleday.)

Lurçat, Jean. *Designing Tapestry.* Rockhill, (London), 1950.

McLendon, Verda L. "Removing Stains from Fabrics." Home and Garden Bulletin 62. U.S. Department of Agriculture. Government Printing Office. (15¢)

Nicolaïdes, Kimon. *The Natural Way to Draw.* Houghton Mifflin, 1941.

Prerau, Sidney. *Taxes and the Craftsman.* American Craft Council Guidebook for Members, 1964.

Quinn, Richard L. "Carpets and Rugs." Hoover Home Institute, 1971.

Slivka, Rose, et al. *The Crafts of the Modern World.* Horizon, 1968.

Tidball, Harriett. "Color and Dyeing." Monograph 1665. Shuttle Craft Guild, 1965. (Distributed by Craft and Hobby Book Service, Big Sur, Calif.)

Wells, George. "Hooking with a Punch Needle." Pamphlet.

———."How to Dye Meriwell Acidified Yarns in Craftsman's Dyes." Pamphlet.

Willcox, Donald J. *Techniques of Rya Knotting.* Van Nostrand, 1971.

Wiseman, Ann. *Rag Rugs and Wool Pictures.* Scribner's, 1968.

———. *Rag Tapestries and Wool Mosaics.* Van Nostrand, 1969.

Zarbock, Barbara J. *The Complete Book of Rug Hooking.* 2nd ed. Van Nostrand, 1969.

Znamierowski, Nell. *Step by Step Rugmaking.* Golden Press, 1972.

Index

Notes

Notes